On sentry duty

Gara-Yaka

THE STORY OF A CHEETAH

by Desmond Varaday

NEW YORK: E. P. DUTTON & CO., INC.: 1964

I AM GRATEFUL to Willie Schürman and his family of Pretoria—fellow cheetah lovers—whose unselfish cooperation was a great encouragement and contributed in no small measure to the completion of the story.

In addition, I express my indebtedness to my bush-loving friends and Wild Life enthusiasts, whose interest was always a source of inspiration.

Not least, I wish to thank those photographers who so willingly provided me with pictures, enriching the illustrations with their work. Their names are credited in the list of illustrations.

To MARYJANE, *my wife,*
whose help made this book come to life

illustrations

Color Plates

Gara-Yaka

chapter 1

THERE IS A wonderland of wild bush country in the triangle of the Shashi and Limpopo Rivers—a broad wedge which forms the east border of the Bechuanaland Protectorate where I was warden of a private reserve. This 50 square miles of territory is a wild-life paradise, with roaming herds of elephant, led by venerable old bulls with almost 200 pounds of ivory in their huge tusks; eland, kudu, and impala mix with troops of zebra and wildebeest, while the great hunting-cats live here in luxury on Nature's fully stocked larder.

Dangers await the unwary, and often the four-footed hunters become the hunted too—as on that late afternoon at the Limpopo when I was taking water-level readings on marked poles near the shore.

An almost imperceptible furrow on the water's surface gave the signal. The movement was directly ahead near a pole in deeper water, and could only have been caused by the tail of a crocodile. This was no unusual occurrence, for nearly all of Africa's waters house crocodiles, but in this case I hastily withdrew to the bank, for by the way the murky water churned under that furrow, it was clear that a huge reptile lurked there, a menace to any living creature that might venture to the water's edge.

While I made the requisite notes on the readings, some 30 yards upwind a magnificent cheetah stepped out of cover, testing the wind with high-held shiny nose. Satisfied, it walked obliquely down to where I had been only a few minutes earlier.

Then as the cheetah slowly lapped up water, it found itself looking into the glassy yellow-green eyes of the huge crocodile, which had been approaching the shore since it had first seen me. The cheetah uttered a sharp bird-like cry of surprise.

For one instant the flat nose and the eyes of the reptile looked like any of the numerous small rocks pitting the water's surface; in the next, there was a terrible commotion as the crocodile sped through the narrow space of shallows separating it from its intended victim. The great wide mouth opened in a loathsome caricature of a smile, and then the jagged teeth clamped together over the cheetah's head. The victim never had a chance.

The water boiled during the momentary tug of war. The hapless hunting-cat fought desperately to free itself. But the attacker was dragging it into the water, where it could hold its prize until it drowned.

I lifted my .375 Magnum H.&H. sporting rifle and fired a snap shot at the reptile's head. The crocodile was submerged only a few inches below the surface. Water splashed at the impact and I clearly heard the "flup" of the bullet striking and then the whine of a ricochet.

The monster reared up, dropping the cheetah, and fell backwards into the water with a resounding crack. But it seemed to be dazed only temporarily, for it made its way off rapidly. By the chain fastened to its right armpit, I recognized Mulembe, the sacred crocodile of the Ba-

Mulembe, Terror of the River

Kwena tribe, who, several decades before, used to come out of the water in response to the call of his worshipers to be fed and honored. Long since, however, the tribe had become civilized, leaving Mulembe to provide his own fare.

After the shot, I reloaded at once and ran across the sand to see if I could help the cheetah. It was lying in the shallows—dead. Its head had been terribly mauled by those powerful jaws. I noticed with regret that the cheetah was a nursing mother; her teats were swollen with milk. She had hoped, it seemed, to drink a sundowner before returning to feed her family. Her death was just one of many unrecorded tragedies daily enacted in the wild bush-lands of Africa.

Since cheetahs are clannish animals, living and hunting

in pairs or families, it was likely that the male would automatically take on the task of feeding the cubs if the mother failed to return to the nursery. The only question was whether the cubs were old enough to feed on what the father could provide. I was curious to find out.

The report of my shot brought Freddie, my Tswana tracker, to the spot. He carried the cheetah's carcass to our Land Rover. I was not happy to have it on hand, for cheetahs are Royal Game—protected by law—and to have its pelt around my quarters could have led to unfair conclusions. But then I realized that its head injuries would be visible, and so I had the pelt pegged out to dry in the camp. That was the action which led to our finding the cubs.

On the second night after the tragedy, I awoke to the sound of a plaintive miaow, a cheetah call. Rex, my fox terrier bitch who had recently had a litter, lifted her head and gave a low growl. The cheetah's cry had come from close by. I suspected it was the male calling its dead mate, for these large hunting-cats are very shy and normally avoid a camp.

I must have dropped off to sleep again, because I was awakened now by the eerie moaning wails of hyenas: "Aar-u-ee, aar-u-eee" they complained. The hideous cries came nearer and nearer to the camp. After several minutes of quiet a sudden burst of savage snarling, growls, and cat-like spitting rent the night air. In half a minute it was over. All was silent. But not for long. There came a fresh outburst—this time wilder.

Taking my flashlight and my rifle I went out, Rex following. There was a wild rush of shadowy forms; eyes shone green in the flashlight beam; then came the crazy laughter-like howl of disturbed hyenas: "Ti-tatata, tita-tatata."

Spotted hyenas, scavengers of the night

A yellowish body dashed through the grass and out of sight. It was a large cheetah: there was no mistaking its long-legged bound and long thick tail. Rex rushed into the scrub to scare away the hyenas who appeared intent on stealing the dead cheetah's pelt which the male had apparently been defending.

At sunrise we read the spoors—the newsprint of the bush—and saw that the cheetah had come upon the scent of his missing mate, approached the camp while calling to her, and at lack of response had come into the camp and found her pegged-out pelt. In the meantime hyenas had also come on the scent.

Two or three hungry hyenas together often become daring, as these had. Many a time they had passed through camp at night snatching away biltong, fleshy oddments and supper left-overs, bones and even old skins. This time there was a fierce guardian to keep them from the drying pelt.

In the scuffle the cheetah had obviously received a bite, for on his spoor we found drops of blood. Freddie (an

Gara-Yaka's father

expert in bushcraft), Rex, and I followed the spoor on foot. We must have gone nearly five miles into gradually thinning bush, losing the spoor, then finding it again, before we came upon a wide depression in the ground. It was densely covered with tall green grass. In the middle of the depression stood a solitary Marula tree. Freddie indicated the tree with his eyes. We stood and listened— to the unmistakable squeals of hungry cubs. This was the cheetah's lair.

A "Koto-koto"—yellow-billed hornbill—was sitting on one of the high branches. When we moved forward, it gave the alarm. I saw the father cheetah slink away from the lair to draw us off the track of the cubs. At the same instant the Koto-koto winged off, protesting loudly at our intrusion.

The long grass, fallen leaves, and dead branches under the Marula tree did not afford a hiding place for a pair of grown cheetahs, but the cubs were so well hidden by a branch that, but for Rex, we would probably not have found them. They must have heard the fall of our steps, for they lay still and silent—a litter of three.

A few feet away on a clear patch there were small mounds of chewed meat, evidently regorged by the father. None of the mounds appeared to have been touched. For lack of teats and mother's milk, the parent instinctively did what he thought the next best thing. But such food was for cubs many weeks older than these.

I realized that although the father was trying, he would be unable to save the cubs, and so I decided to take them. By their size and unspotted tawny gray-colored fur, we judged them to be no more than a couple of weeks old. They had not received nourishment now for over two days, and as I picked up two of them it was obvious that they were famished, for they were as light as bundles of feathers.

I made Rex lie down beside the cubs, and I put the three starved orphans to her teats. As soon as the cubs began to swarm on her, nuzzling her underside hungrily, Rex lifted her lips in a warning snarl. I stroked her and cajoled, and at length my words and possibly her motherly instinct got the better of her repulsion for the strange litter. She let the cubs suckle. For a while only noisy feeding was heard.

One of the three, the only female cub, appeared to be the liveliest and fiercest of them all. She had emptied a teat and highhandedly fought one and then the other of her brothers for possession of the remaining milk faucets.

She succeeded in getting them, too. I had to laugh at her antics, and, despite her sex, there and then named her Cheeky Charlie. Freddie shook his head in disapproval of the name.

While we carried the cubs back to camp, I wondered whether Rex was sufficiently equipped to cope with three additional boarders. Her two healthy pups were always ravenous and there was possibly not enough milk for the newcomers.

Once home, Rex refused absolutely to accept the duties of foster mother. So I had to adopt them and care for the orphans. I groomed them by brushing out their matted fur and wiping them over with a warm, damp cloth. We fed the brood every two hours on powdered milk mixed with water and administered with an eyedropper. It was a long and tedious performance, because we had only one dropper. By the time I had completed the round, the first one was almost due for another feed. It was a full-time job.

To remedy the unavoidable running stomachs, I mixed finely powdered charcoal with the milk and added a pinch of bismuth. Diarrhea, however, got the upper hand. I then resorted to chlorodine, the taste of which did not quite make feeding an unqualified success.

Cheeky Charlie had the "I want to live" instinct and the stronger constitution of a female. She took to the artificial nourishment and, in a way, flourished. Her brothers barely existed and began to look dehydrated and scruffy. I had fears for their survival.

In fact, from the very first day I had doubts about the smaller of the two. After a few days, while feeding him I found that the milk was coming back through his nostrils. On examining his mouth I noticed that he had something like a cleft palate which diverted much of every pull of food to his nose. In the second week he died.

Rex still determinedly refused to assist with the feeding. At night she would stealthily remove her pups from the basket, leaving the squeaking cheetah cubs to huddle together for communal warmth. When this warmth proved insufficient, the cubs protested loudly, waking me. I gave Rex a dark look but she always pretended a deep sleep, though I knew she was shamming. Eventually there was nothing to do but to take the cubs into bed with me. One at a time I popped them under the blanket and pushed them down to my feet. When they were snug I would try to continue the broken night's rest. They remained quiet and slept, pressed against my feet. The nights were getting colder.

Food was the all-important commodity for my fluffy pair, and they made their demands known as long as they were awake. Freddie shared the duties of feeding because I could no longer cope alone. One day, he took one of the cubs out of the basket and stood holding it in his arm while putting the feeder, a lemonade bottle fitted with a rubber teat, to the cub's mouth. The hungry little thing lunged forward and slipped from Freddie's grasp, falling with a dull thud on the hard floor. Its tender young body was internally injured, and after that it refused all food. In spite of our efforts to nurse it back to health, it faded away. Both Freddie and I were very upset at the loss of the cub.

I have never heard of cheetahs breeding in captivity and it seemed that even those born in the wilds were difficult to rear.

Now the only survivor was the female: still as lively and demanding as on the first day. She accepted the feed-

Piet and Freddie with the pups

ing device as naturally as though it were the real thing,
wrapping her tongue around the teat and holding the
bottle with forepaws, purring and suckling contentedly
on it long after it was empty, like an old man sucking a
pipe. She allowed only me to feed her, spitting and striking out at all who came near her.

I suppose the name Cheeky Charlie would have remained hers had not a primitive, disheveled specimen—a
detribalized Bushman—arrived at my camp to seek em-
ployment as a game scout. I was busy feeding the little
cub when Freddie escorted the man to me. As no African
is more cunning in the craft of tracking than a Bushman,
I engaged him. The way Piet looked at the cub convinced
me immediately that he was a keen animal-lover and had
a passion for handling wild game. Respectfully he asked
permission to stroke the cub; this I granted.

But Piet had hardly reached out to stroke the cub's
head when she spat at him so fiercely and loudly that he
instinctively withdrew his hand. He laughed at the

savagery of the small unspotted fur-ball, and also at his own fright. "Ow!" he exclaimed. "This is Gara-Yaka, mother of the monsters and the ghosts that walk by night!"

And from then on she was called Gara-Yaka. In a short while her ears became so attuned to the sound of this name that she answered to no other.

In a playful mood

chapter 2

SOMEHOW REX had become less harsh to the lone cub. She even permitted the cheetah to share the family basket. I was surprised to find Gara-Yaka also sharing Rex's milk with the pups, but she condescended to accept this belated hospitality only during the daytime. The nights she still spent with me, snuggled under the bedclothes, occasionally coming up for air.

Soon she was running and gamboling around with the pups, an absolute picture of health and happiness, scratching at fleas as vigorously as the dogs did. She had learned how to ask to be picked up: she would stretch her long arms, place them on me, and look until I gathered her up.

At three months Gara-Yaka was big. She appropriated the dog basket, using it as her daytime apartment. She was always quick to mete out punishment to the dogs if they ventured too near the comfortable basket.

My pet was by now a cuddlesome, feline beauty, with long gangling dog legs. She was a strange mixture of dog and cat. Polka dots were becoming clearly defined on her tawny, golden hide. The fur on her rounded belly was creamy, the texture of swan's-down.

As on grown cheetahs, Gara-Yaka's head was her most typical feature. The lyre-shaped black lines were already fully marked on her cheeky face, starting at the inner corners of her eyes and ending at her upper lip, where, like badly applied make-up, the "tear-stain" became smudged and lost in the growing whiskers. She was still quite fluffy, and her loose coat was well padded with puppy-fat. By the day she grew more affectionate.

At about this time she began serious bouts of hide-and-seek with her stepbrothers. It was mostly she who stalked. Instinct gave her the know-how. The game usually ended with a rush and a charge in which the pups were caught at a hopeless disadvantage. They rolled over with stumbling clumsiness. But there were times when they came on Gara-Yaka unexpectedly, and this scared her. I noticed that she was easily frightened. On these occasions, she would rise to her full height, get up on her toes, arch her back, and stretch her tail out stiff, its hairs bristling like a bottle brush, and then hop sideways, stiff-legged. Then she would get even with the pups by spitting at them and cuffing them repeatedly. At times when they charged her she raced up a tree like a cat, still with that wild look in her eyes.

This appeared to be the age for ratifying established relationships. She spat and growled at all Bantu except Freddie and Piet, whom she accepted as part and parcel of the camp.

To all intents and purposes I was still Mama, and this was confirmed daily when she clambered into my lap while I was relaxing. She would creep up to my chest and lie there, purring in a strange, deep, throaty gurgle and "making puddings"—kneading me with her semi-retractile claws. Then the real caressing would begin: she would

She loved chin-chucking

rub her face against my cheeks and gaze into my eyes. In bright sunlight her large eyes shone like polished jasper.

Her attitude toward Rex became very frivolous, and gradually she looked upon the mother dog as an equal. In spite of the dog's cool superiority and occasional chastisement—in what seemed to be a last effort on Rex's part to establish her waning authority—the cheetah accepted no such discipline.

When Gara-Yaka was with the dogs, she considered herself one of them, even trying to behave like them. She learned everything and did everything the dogs could do, except bark. Her voice remained that of a big cat.

Then there were times when Gara-Yaka behaved like a human baby, especially when she lay on my chest. She made no secret of her own belief that I was still Mother, and that she lived only to love me. I had noticed this very deep affection among wild cheetahs, who, at the finish of a meal, with much ado, lick each other's face clean and then lie sleeping with arms and legs entwined like human lovers.

My cheetah did this to her foster brothers, who, although visibly disliking this sort of familiarity, put up with it for the sake of peace, while lifting their lips in a warning grimace. Gara-Yaka would have one or the other pup by the throat and gently but firmly squeeze her jaws together to force the pup to accept whatever she was meting out. The happy family circle would then break up with much squealing and howling on the part of the dogs. At this, Gara-Yaka would be thoroughly fed up with the unsporting attitude of the pups and come join me. She was obviously self-willed and independent, her wild heritage showing through her every act.

Wherever I went, she came too. I had no choice, for she would follow anyway. The moment she opened her eyes in the morning, she would greet me with an affectionate whistle-like meouw. She shared my tea, lapping out of my saucer, but if I was too slow pouring hers first, she would firmly but politely remind me of my negligence by placing her paw on the tray, almost upsetting it. Even when the saucer was empty, she made quite sure that no dregs were left: she held it firm while she ran her tongue over it looking for the last drop, tea leaves and all.

Eventually, Gara-Yaka was weaned from her liquid diet to solids. At the first attempt I chopped the meat finely for her. To my consternation she would not even look at it. Taking a leaf from her father's book, I chewed raw liver for her, but achieved similar results. The raw offal tasted horrible, but anything for a good cause!

Patiently I dipped my finger into the chewed bloody mess and smeared it across her lips. Surprisingly she took my finger in her mouth and sucked off the blood. This maneuver, repeated three or four times, comprised the meal. Later I purposely dropped minced liver on the floor. She picked up the small lumps, and from then on she took to raw meat almost eagerly. Her survival as a carnivore was thus assured.

She had acquired the habit of resting her forepaws on my shoulders during mealtimes, breathing down my neck. This was all very well while she limited herself to inactive participation, but once in a while she would reach forward with her paw to clobber whatever morsel took her fancy. She did not stop there. The next thing she did was to swipe every mouthful from my fork. Unfortunately for her, once the meat was piping hot and it burned her tender paw. After this my meals were somewhat less disturbed, but she seemed to look at me accusingly, as though she thought I had purposely done that hurtful thing to her.

When she had grown her full set of teeth, I fed her on lumps of raw meat dipped in cod-liver oil. Now and then I gave her a chunk with bone. She took to it eagerly, tearing the meat from the bone with her scissor-sharp teeth, swallowing the lumps without chewing. She did try to crack the bones, but since her teeth were less power-

ful than those of a lion or a leopard, she failed with the
larger ones.

After she had dined well, her paunch showed a rounded
fullness. She would flop over under her favorite bush,
yawn, and doze off into a deep drugged sleep. Gara-Yaka
nevertheless adored the sunshine, and spent far more time
sunning herself than a bathing beauty. Often she would
awaken quite suddenly from a deep sleep, and commence
a delightful feline ballet with her tennis ball.

Her sense of hearing was so acute that the crawl of a
beetle could stir her to watchfulness. The hearing was
complemented by an excellent power of smell. Being intel-
ligently curious, she often stood "in the wind," sniffling,
classifying, and memorizing the various scents she had
picked up, and which for humans, and often even for
dogs, were beyond detection.

All moving things held a fascination for her. She did
not rest until she had investigated and filed away her im-
pressions and opinions. Her small squarish face was a
study in itself when she came across a new scent. The
heavy brows would knit and the rounded, lion-like ears
would prick forward; the satin of her muzzle shone wet
in the sun, and her reactions to the scent indicated whether
she classified it as friendly or otherwise.

The "food smells" of the various antelope added an
almost fierce expression to the typical contemplative look
of her kind. While scenting, she twitched and jerked the
tasseled end of her tail, and if she smelled a fellow carnivore—cousin lion or leopard, for instance—it usually disturbed or angered her. She would utter a deep "Ungh," a
short and rather hoarse growl, more in warning than with
menace.

Once we came upon a grown cheetah hunting upwind
from us. I had long been curious to know her reaction to

Gara-Yaka at four months

such an event. Gara-Yaka seemed to fill her lungs joyously
with the scent of this relative. Her chest expanded fully
and she gave the characteristic high-pitched chirping
sound, at which, to her surprise, the cheetah made off.

But while the tame and the wild had briefly eyed each
other, I must admit that my heart had beat a little faster.
That was a moment of decision, for the lure to be with
her own kind must have been strong indeed, and I had
watched the outcome with mixed feelings.

By now Gara-Yaka and I were inseparable pals, and it
would have pained me had she jilted me in the bush.
Despite her visible surprise at the strange flight of her
relative, my cheetah appeared to be happy that she had
remained with me—and so was I. Fully realizing that I
should encourage her to return to the life to which she was
born, I had left the choice to her. Now she rubbed against
my legs, smiling, her tail held high, probably reassuring
me of her love. She brushed her whiskers on my toes, her
favorite way of expressing devotion. All was well still.

At heart and in habit she was no more than a cub,
for in spite of her rapid growth, her whole life was a game
of stalk and rush at imaginary objects and a big pretense of
living wild. She started to practice hunting on hornbills,
barbets, and doves. Watching them alight from trees to
search for food, she would creep very low on her belly,
brushing the ground, taking advantage of every bush,
stone, and literally even a blade of grass. Closer and closer
she would creep, not realizing that the sharp eyes of the
birds had noted her presence. By the time Gara-Yaka was
ready to leap, the bird had risen and was already settling
on the branch of the nearest tree, swearing at the cheetah
from the safety of its perch.

Gara-Yaka returned from these adventures like a chastised schoolgirl whose homework had been ill prepared. I

always pretended to be busy with something so as not to make it obvious that I had witnessed her failure. I would give her a dog biscuit as compensation, and this never failed to dispel the gloom of her disappointment. She had developed a great passion for dog biscuits and would leave any of her regular pleasure routines when she heard my call to the dogs, "Come-see, come-see," which meant biscuit-time.

No amount of failure could demoralize Gara-Yaka. She received her first lessons in bushcraft from Rex, but already she far outdid the old teacher. I was fortunate to witness my cheetah's first successful hunt. Her quarry was one of those teasing Koto-kotos, probably one she had failed to catch when she was still slow and clumsy. She had noted the bird's routine. But this time the tree of refuge chosen by the bird happened to be one with a sloping trunk. Instead of turning back disappointed when she flushed the bird, she continued her rush up the tree, and before the surprised bird could settle on a branch, Gara-Yaka had it.

But her first success was not all victory. My cheetah had from time to time run up slightly sloping trees, whether with or without the aid of her claws, I could not say. Unlike her cousins, the great cats whose claws are retractile, hers are only half retractable, but not as stiffly set as those of a dog. Cheetahs sometimes use their dew-claws to get a hold on the back of a hunted antelope before bringing it down. Often they scratch the bark of certain trees they pick out as gathering spots. And they help pivot themselves on their claws when taking a purchase on the ground in their speedy chase of quarry. Claws or not, Gara-Yaka came a cropper with her first catch. Holding the Koto-koto in her jaws, she overshot a branch and came to earth with a hollow flop.

I closed my eyes, expecting the worst. But within seconds I felt her brushing against my legs, tail up and purring in that deep satisfied tone she used when she was pleased. Her jasper eyes spoke volumes. In ten minutes she ate the bird, feathers and all, except the long wings.

With this adventure began a new phase in the life of my cheetah. Often she would take off from a standing start and outrush any bird before it had time to rise high enough, clawing it out of the air. Butterflies and potbellied beetles buzzing by were an irresistible challenge, and she usually caught them if she really meant to, for cheetahs are the fastest creatures on earth.

The speed of cheetahs has been variously put at between 60 and 84 miles an hour—the latter figure clocked with a stopwatch on a greyhound track. I once tried to race a family of five cheetahs to test their speed. When I came upon them, I was on an open stretch of dirt road with scarcely a winding. For the most part, bush roads twist and turn and are very uneven and rough. Often it is risky to exceed 30 m.p.h.

The family was about to cross the road when I happened along. They veered off and continued running parallel with the road. I stepped on the gas and watched the needle rise rapidly from 25 m.p.h. while the family also accelerated, going gradually faster and faster.

We sped along neck and neck, the cheetahs flat out and yet not looking at all strained. Their smooth stretch-and-fold gait was like the tautening and relaxing of a rubber band and, in comparison, nearest to the greyhound's style of running. I glanced at the speedometer; the needle hovered around 60. Whether they could have made it faster I am unable to say, but, I reiterate, they did not look at all strained.

We had reached the end of the open road and much to

my regret I had to slow down. It would have been looking for trouble had I driven faster than 20 m.p.h. on the next stretch, as I knew well from the experience of some close friends of mine.

They had slid fast around a particularly sharp turning one day and had come to a sudden but cushioned halt against the posterior of an elephant. Fortunately they traveled in a closed jeep or they could have come to harm. As it was, they had to sit and listen, terror-stricken, to the infuriated elephant's trumpeting. They watched petrified as its ears flapped menacingly and it stamped holes in the ground. It was a miracle that the animal did not become violent. After what seemed hours to them, the elephant turned and walked off into the bush, trunk still raised, tail swishing and ears flapping. My friends sighed with relief and thanked The One responsible for the elephant's change of heart!

Anyway, no sooner had I slowed down than the cheetah family cut across my path and ran forward to a large tree beside the road. There, panting, they lay down. One of them suddenly rose, smelled the trunk of the tree, walked forward about ten feet, and made water like a tomcat, hitting the tree squarely with unerring feline marksmanship.

Unfortunately the urgency of my journey prevented further lingering. Such a gathering—five cheetahs together—was a very rare sight.

chapter 3

My permanent camp was near a place called Sparkling Waters. Crystal-clear pure water bubbled out from underneath large slabs of flat, sloping rocks. The place was thinly wooded with large Camelthorn and Ironwood trees and three or four enormous Baobab—Cream-of-Tartar trees. Beyond my camp limits began the thick Mopani bush.

Under one of the thorn trees grew a tangle of scrub and long grass. This was the home of a covey of crested francolin. Every morning they greeted the rising sun or said farewell to the setting with their characteristic call and clucking, which according to a prominent ornithologist sounds like "I'll drink yer beer." This call they repeat three times, thereby giving away their hiding place. It was their musical birdcall that was one of the first of many bush sounds that made Gara-Yaka take notice.

Now, having graduated as a hunter, she decided to have a try at catching these birds. Francolin are extremely wily if they can hide, but when flushed they break into a confused whirr of chirping and run on open ground as fast as a rocket.

Whether or not there exists a common animal language

is a point to be pondered, but different animals certainly do communicate with each other. At one sunset Rex went to flush out our francolins for Gara-Yaka. My cheetah skirted downwind of the birds and sheltered behind a grass tuft which camouflaged her so well she became almost invisible.

The dog had done a good job of flushing, and the covey was pouring out of the tangle, running hell-for-leather and protesting for all they were worth. Gara-Yaka shot out and caught one of the rocketing birds as though it were a sitting duck.

This game of hunting was repeated daily by the two until the confused covey was annihilated. Cheetahs usually hunt in pairs or in families. This instinct must have prompted Gara-Yaka to join Rex, but I would still like to know how they made arrangements for the combined operations and how the role of each was assigned. Beater and hunter? They even shared the resultant feast!

My animals hunted because of instinct, not because they were hungry. Rex was born on a cattle ranch deep in the wilds and was as much a part of the bush as a wild lion or antelope or, for that matter, Gara-Yaka herself. I encouraged this hunting, for it gave my young cheetah the necessary practice to provide for herself in the event of her deciding to leave home. A semi-experienced cheetah might survive alone and I daresay because of its inborn instinct does not need special training as lions probably do.

It is a strange fact that although parts of the bush may teem with game, an inexperienced carnivore might well be on the border of starvation. It should be remembered that the impala, the "daily bread" of the hunting-cats, generally gather in herds from August to March. These herds post sentinels which are very alert and at the least suspicion sound the alarm with short hoarse snorts.

Impala ram on sentry duty

The sentinels seek the open or elevated positions from which they can watch a particular patch of cover that appears to house some suspected danger. As soon as the alarm is given, the whole herd is on the alert, and as many pairs of eyes scan the approaches as there are animals in the herd. Consequently it is not easy, even for the very experienced great cats, to stalk up close to the herd unless rugged terrain or bushes permit this. Thus they prefer to wait in ambush.

The alarm soon subsides and the herd resumes its grazing while frequently the sentinels advance toward the thicket where they stop, look, and listen for any danger sign. When quite near the bush they will suddenly veer and run in mock retreat, to try to induce an inexperienced predator to disclose its whereabouts.

At first Gara-Yaka fell for their ruse, and so frequently found herself in the midst of madly leaping impala, which made jumps of 20 feet or more, like a school of giant grasshoppers, for a couple of moments, and then ran swiftly to a distance of 40 or 50 yards, from which spot they could look back at the cheetah, left bewildered by the lack of a specific quarry.

Once, after several such lessons, Gara-Yaka rushed into the middle of a herd that was retiring with prodigious leaps. She made a jet-propelled charge. It was grand to watch her streak in a beeline for a selected animal—a little ewe—and pass several of the laggards on the way. But a peculiar thing happened. Having reached her quarry Gara-Yaka suddenly found herself face to face with a young lioness hunting the same animal! Such a coincidence is not rare in the bush.

During my cheetah's charge I had noticed two large lions silently emerge from the bush to the left of the impala herd, endeavoring to drive the herd toward my right where, unknown to the impala, to Gara-Yaka, and to me, two mature and two young lionesses were cleverly concealed in the undergrowth. These four now dashed out of cover with the usual leonine velocity, and in a split second the mature lionesses had pulled down two rams and a young lion got Gara-Yaka's little ewe. I am sorry that I was not close enough to observe the faces of my cheetah and her lioness opponent. There must have been surprised looks on both sides.

The young lioness, the more ferocious of the two hunters, was indeed the owner of the kill. She coughed a string of deep warning grunts and slunk down as though to leap. Gara-Yaka with a spiteful hiss sank back with flattened ears, then instantly pivoted forward on her long hind legs, cuffed the lioness on the ear and again on the face. I winced, horrified. Fighting cats!

In my mind's eye I could see the melee that usually follows this sort of beginning. But I was as proud of my cheetah as I had been of myself when, years before, I hit a bullying schoolboy much bigger than I and brought him to his knees.

Much has been said for and against the opinion that animals help each other, and I agree with both sides. I once saw a lioness looking casually at a sister huntress six feet away who had attacked a rather large wildebeest bull. The huntress had made a bad charge and was hanging onto the muzzle of the bull, which was standing firmly on all fours. She lay powerless on her back between the bull's forelegs. Both were helpless. Had the watching lioness helped her sister, they would surely have made the kill, but she simply looked on.

Three or four minutes passed and the lioness and wildebeest remained locked motionless. Then the lioness suddenly released her hold. The bull jumped aside, bucked, and not overhastily trotted back to join his herd which had stood by silently watching the drama a few hundred yards away. The lioness slowly walked back to her hiding place like a whipped dog, obviously feeling very ashamed at her failure.

A contrast to this incident was the occasion when two elephant bulls, like good samaritans, propped up and helped away a third bull of their own size which I had shot. Holding him between them, they supported his bulk till he eventually dropped. Then they stood beside him with expressions of "We have failed you."

Now, however, it seemed Gara-Yaka was going to have trouble with the two young lionesses, for the sister was coming to join my cheetah's adversary, either for support or perhaps only to share the kill. I decided not to take a

chance, and with Freddie and Piet I shouted to the cheetah
to come. Rex, so far silent, now broke into furiously
hysterical barking.

For a moment the lionesses stood as though frozen, and
for that little time, they were an impressive sight. Gara-
Yaka took her cue and bounded back to us with all the
leonine eyes hard on her retreating figure. Since we had
no business to intrude we speedily withdrew, and looking
back saw the lions dragging their prey into thicker bush
for a long and quiet feed.

Gara-Yaka appeared to be less shaken than we, for the
only sign of excitement she showed was the way she held
her whipping tail high. She did not even consider the lions
worthy of a backward glance as we left the scene.

chapter 4

GARA-YAKA HAD the domestic habit of playing with shoes and slippers. She would thrust one of her forelegs into a shoe or, preferably, under the crossed straps of an open sandal, then feel around. Undoubtedly, in her mind this was a great game. At times she pushed both forelegs neatly into the two sandals placed side by side, and she did look comical!

After months of such play she took it upon herself to be guardian of my footwear. Against whom or what she guarded them remained her secret. She lay curled up like a snail or stretched out like a sphinx near a pair of shoes, just watching. When Rex or the pups ventured near by chance or on purpose, Gara-Yaka pulled down her heavy eyebrows and scowled at the intruder, the way a jealous lover might look at a rival.

At these times her eyes took on a hard, stiff look. The intruders made off at once, clearly understanding her expression. I have found that animals of different species, especially the feline and canine families, do communicate with each other at times, soundlessly, simply by looking.

Whether the look was friendly, disinterested, or outright dangerous, it was never misinterpreted.

When the dogs brazenly ignored her warning look or did not take sufficient notice, Gara-Yaka lifted her upper lip high, showing a mouthful of perfect teeth in a threatening grimace. This always had the desired effect.

I, in my dim blundering human way, once ignored her refusal to give up my slippers and took them regardless of the consequences. She clouted my arm hard, tearing my sleeve and drawing blood. Naturally, I retaliated. Tit-for-tat settled this misunderstanding between us and we were both sorry. A good deal of purring and licking, patting and cuddling re-established the status quo.

My cheetah bitterly resented chastisement in any form, though it seemed she was more offended than angered. After a mild scolding which, in the words of parents, "hurt me as much," Gara-Yaka would take a pair of my footwear out of camp and, guarding them, would sit for many hours, probably brooding over the cruel life she lived.

Puppies have the habit of taking away a shoe, a sock, or almost any article of clothing to play with and to chew. Then, when something else attracts their attention, they drop and forget the article. But not so with Gara-Yaka. She unfailingly brought back what she had removed.

One day about mid-afternoon, Gara-Yaka came to my hut carrying the soft-soled leather shoes which I generally use for silent walking in the bush. In these shoes, provided I am downwind from the game, I can stalk and approach very close to animals I wish to observe.

My cheetah had just put down the shoes when I heard the distant "Blam" of a heavy-caliber rifle. The season for hunting was closed, since most of the antelope ewes and other female game were looking forward to "happy events."

Certain farm owners to the south and west had shooting rights at any time on their own properties, but the shot had come from the northwest, beyond privately owned land. Poachers! The word echoed through my mind. Freddie and Piet reported immediately at my open door and confirmed the shot and its direction.

Hastily I pulled on my bush-clothes and reached out for one of my shoes. Contrary to my habit of first shaking out my shoes, I pushed my foot in. There was an awful fraction of a second while my toes investigated an obstruction in the shoe. Such a moment appears much longer because of the suspense attached to it.

Through sheer reflex I jerked off the shoe and flung it out of the hut. As it turned in the air, I saw the "obstruction" fly out. It was an adult black scorpion about four inches long! The creature fell to a small rock outcrop where it immediately took up a fighting position. The knobby tail came up in a semicircle with its curved sting pointing forward in readiness.

Gara-Yaka had witnessed the whole happening and, curious as usual, ran toward the scorpion. I have never come across a wild animal stung by a scorpion, so I could not gauge what the consequences might be if Gara-Yaka ventured too close. The sting of this big black scorpion is highly dangerous and has proved fatal in humans. I have always had the greatest respect for them. I rushed out to hold back my inquisitive ward and thought I would try to crush the black horror.

It seemed I was unduly worried, for the scorpion's fighting stance was not directed at us! Even before I reached the flat rock I saw a dry grass-root-like object lying on it and this suddenly became animated. It proved to be a huge sun-spider, deadly enemy of the black scorpion. This queer long-bodied spider grows to between four and six

inches in length, including its long hairy legs. It loves the
sun and can be found lying as though dead on rocks or
stones which are almost too hot to be touched by hand.

Without a referee's whistle, the two deadly contestants
rushed at one another. They gripped and danced, crawled
and tumbled round and round each other, each managing
to get in a bite. They kept up this deadly contest for several
moments—a dance macabre. Then they both died! As suddenly as they mete out death, so they die when at the
receiving end.

chapter 5

YES, DEATH IS very quick in the bush—the way Nature
administers it—but slow and agonizing sometimes when it
comes by the hand of man.

There was a little-used path leading northwestward.
Both my trackers knew these parts well, and both of them
had taken the job with me for sheer love of the bush and
its denizens. Freddie and Piet were simple people, but
their hearts were in the right place. They strongly opposed
the brutal slaughter of game, although both, like myself,
had previously been keen hunters. They hated the suffering
caused by the underhanded methods used by native
poachers in their unceasing quest for meat.

Freddie assured me that he had pinpointed the area
where the shot had come from. He and I sat in the Land
Rover's front seat with Gara-Yaka between us. Ever since
her lap-cub days, she had sat with me in front, and as she
grew, this habit became firmly established. She was able to
see more of the passing bush from this position. Now she
sat in dog fashion on her haunches, her front legs straight
with paws neatly placed together. Her jasper eyes peered
eagerly ahead. Piet was in the back.

Freddie stopped me at a particularly broken part of the bush where a trail forked off. We left the Land Rover on the path and struck out northward into thick bush. Driving would have been precarious here for the ground was scored with dongas and washouts which, in rainy weather, drained away the water to the now dry sandbed of the Majali River.

Like a hunting dog, Gara-Yaka ran ahead of us. Long before the sharp eyes of my trackers saw game, my cheetah stiffened and sank to her haunches, indicating the presence of animals or birds. Although at times her wonderful camouflage made her quite invisible, we could usually guess where she was by the way the game stared at a bush or a grass patch. All horned game ran as soon as they detected her.

We had probably gone a mile when Gara-Yaka returned to us. She was behaving in a strange manner, as though afraid, rubbing hard against my legs, wanting to stop me from advancing. We seldom spoke in the bush, and so far our movements had been as soundless as careful walking permitted. Freddie raised his eyebrows and indicated the direction in which we were heading. It seemed he wanted us to pay attention to Gara-Yaka's warning.

We did, for only a hundred yards further on my cheetah drew behind a bush, lay down, and growled under her breath. It was the type of throaty growl she used when the pups approached my shoes or when there were strangers in the camp. She raised her muzzle high and sniffed the air. Judging by these signs there were natives and probably dogs in the vicinity.

We listened carefully but nothing unusual was audible. The bush seems silent, but its symphony plays on constantly. Crickets chirp, green luries squawk, shrikes rattle, hornbills honk, and the wood doves coo. Above all these sounds is the buzz of the cheeky, blue carrion flies swarming around one's eyes, ears, and nostrils, all the while giving out a high-pitched whine, making a nuisance of themselves.

The path we had been following was a defined game-trail, and we now continued in single file, led by Freddie. Gara-Yaka again trotted a few yards ahead, and then she suddenly went head-over-heels and up in the air—her long legs haywire. She was suspended by one leg and hung struggling and helpless.

Piet, Freddie, and I immediately jumped to pull down the springy sapling to the top of which a length of piano wire had been fixed, terminating in a running noose. Gara-Yaka dangled from this noose which had closed tight around her right foreleg, the wire cutting deep into the skin. Freddie and Piet made an effort to lift her, so that I might release the noose. But Gara-Yaka was in a frenzy; she bit at her leg and at our hands. From a "tame cat" she had been instantly transformed into a mad wild beast. Though it did not take long to release her, I do not think she ever quite forgot this unfortunate experience with the cruel wire snare.

When we could again concentrate on our mission, we heard the faint but unmistakable sound of wood-chopping in the distance. Sound travels well in the bush, and it was not difficult to guess that the persons responsible for setting the snare were not far away, preparing and laying more of their infernal contraptions.

The chopped-off crown of the springy sapling that had supplied the traction power for the snare lay close by and the leaves on it were not yet withered. It seemed that a line or series of traps were in the course of construction. Had it not been for the shot, we might have remained completely unaware of these devilish activities. I pacified

Gara-Yaka, for she was shaking nervously, and we advanced more cautiously.

Not far ahead we quite suddenly came on a party of five natives. They were shocked when I stepped out into view and challenged them. Their eyes showed white against their shiny, sweaty skins. They would have made off, but Freddie and Piet made an encircling move. I fired a warning shot into the air and they surrendered.

Gara-Yaka at my heels, growling her displeasure at the sight of them, seemed to have arrested the attention of the five captives. The leader of the gang brazenly offered me five cattle for her, which, considering that the same would buy a wife, was a very good price. Naturally his offer was firmly turned down. I had other business with these poachers.

"Where's your rifle?" I asked the man.

"Rifle?" he echoed in a tone of outraged innocence. "There's no rifle here, sir. We are poor, starving people gathering firewood."

As the nearest settlement was about 15 miles away, he must have regarded himself a plausible liar or thought me very simple. I looked at the sapling he had been working on when we surprised them: the job was complete.

It was exactly the same type of death trap which had earlier caught Gara-Yaka—a springy sapling bent hard over and fastened to a catch in the ground. The noose is laid so that when a victim puts its foot inside it, the catch is triggered off. The sapling whips back and the noose is pulled tight, jerking the animal off its feet. Ingenious, but deadly and very cruel.

With a stick I released the catch and watched the young tree swish upright; the wire noose pulled the stick from my hand and it dangled in the air. Very few lovers of wild life realize the evil of such snares. A wire snare outdoes every other mode of game destruction, for it catches and kills regardless of age, sex, or type of animal. The snare does not of course kill outright but holds the luckless victim captive till it dies from hunger and thirst. Even a man-eater is more merciful. These spring traps are most effective for the large hunting-cats, especially leopards—whose skin these natives were probably after.

"There's your firewood," I said to the leader, pointing to the stick dangling in the noose. He merely grinned sheepishly, an acknowledgment of guilt. He seemed incapable of realizing the cruelty of his method. "Who fired the shot?" I further questioned him. "No shot, no rifle, sir," he insisted. But I could tell he was lying.

Gara-Yaka lifted her nose high and sniffed the air. She growled. I kicked at a clod of earth to ascertain the direction of the wind by the flying dust. A light breeze blew from where the path dipped down toward a water hole. Gara-Yaka was facing in that direction, growling like a dog at an intruder's scent.

We marched our prisoners down to the water hole. Gara-Yaka led us directly to the freshly skinned and partly dismembered carcass of a water-buck. A quick look around showed the footprints of at least three more poachers with dogs, all of whom had now decamped—or so I thought.

My cheetah had now centered her attention on a thick bush some 60 yards away. She stared so hard at the bush that I decided to investigate. Hardly had I gone five steps with Gara-Yaka following when a tall native stepped from behind a bush. He unhurriedly raised his rifle to his shoulder, took aim, and fired. I heard the slug whistle by about three or four feet to the right.

Covering the would-be murderer with my rifle, I called on him to surrender, warning him that at any wrong move I would shoot. He apparently had more faith in my aim than in his own, for he calmly and sullenly gave himself up and handed over his rifle, an ancient muzzle-loading museum piece. Its wooden stock was chewed out of all recognition by white ants and was held together by tattered rawhide strips, the gun having probably been hidden in the hollow of a tree during its long unlicensed lifetime.

The barrel of the antique firearm was so pockmarked with rust that it stained my hand. Undoubtedly the inside of the barrel was in a similar or possibly even a worse condition. It is almost certain that this gun had been in use since the days of Stanley and Livingstone. I held out my hand for the bullets. He handed me a tobacco bag full of powder—I supposed this was purchased from a trading store—and his bullets. These were two-inch lengths of iron, cut from the kind of thick wire used for the reinforcement of concrete pillars in buildings. How this type of wire found its way into the bush remained a mystery.

Gara-Yaka aided my trackers to look for more snares. We found a complete battery of them waylaying every game-path leading to the water hole. No thirsty animal coming here to drink could have been fortunate enough to avoid getting caught. There were 22 snares altogether: their value very high indeed in poaching communities.

Such a number of snares would have done to death practically as many animals. Strangely, the men who set these abominable gadgets did not look at all like "poor starving people" as the leader claimed. They, in fact, appeared well fed and "shiny," as natives in good physical condition generally look. The meat would have been for trading. They were a band of "won't works"—the type that give trouble to their chiefs.

They had no compunction about disclosing the identity of their decamped colleagues now that they realized the game was up. In due course we collected the other three and the bunch were later sentenced, and their weapons and stocks of wire confiscated.

We took the water-buck back to camp, and after removing some of the meat for my trackers and for myself, I put out the carcass to see what Gara-Yaka would do with it. To my satisfaction, she lay down in the manner of grown cheetahs and began feeding. Her sharp teeth made short work of the tough tendons of the shoulder and breast. After the feed, like a fastidious cat, she washed her face and paws and jumped heavily into my lap, droning her purr of repletion. I felt especially honored when she placed her long gangling arms on either side of my neck and touched the tip of my nose with her icy one in an "Eskimo kiss."

chapter 6

THEN ONE DAY Gara-Yaka refused her food. I inspected the meat which was part of the camp's ration for the day and found it to be perfectly fresh. I wondered if she had supplemented her diet with bird or small buck, but my search for feathers, bones, and skin proved fruitless: there were no telltale remains anywhere near the camp. I went about my tasks in the camp with a growing feeling of uneasiness.

By late afternoon I noticed that my cheetah was becoming less active, and she lay in the hut under my bed rather than on it. I knelt down beside her and felt her nose. It was dry and very warm. This convinced me that Gara-Yaka was ill. However, I tried to dispel my worry by reminding myself that within the hour it would be her feeding time again and maybe then my fears would prove groundless.

I chose a small juicy buck steak and cut it up into cubes, thinking I would hand-feed her and pamper her a little. I tinkled the saucer to summon her to dinner, but she ignored this much-loved signal and remained under the bed, so I took the meat to her. Her jasper eyes seemed

pained, and I spoke, cajoling, begging her to eat. She
turned her head away and I noticed her eyes were running,
wet streaks staining her face on either side of her nose.

Now I was deeply concerned. My mind in a turmoil, I
got up and went out of the hut, thinking hard what to try
next. The sun was already touching the horizon in a blaze
of flame. The whole world seemed to me to be upset.
Freddie, preparing our evening meal, was a welcome sight.
I did not feel so alone.

Freddie listened attentively while I told him of my fears
for Gara-Yaka's well-being. He was immediately concerned.
He suggested that we dose the cheetah with "mutie,"
the native fever-breaking herbs. I welcomed the suggestion,
and he went off in haste to fetch a goodly supply of dried
herbs from his hut. We made a brew and cooled it. Now,
how to administer the stuff!

The cheetah lay in exactly the same position as when
I had left her. Her face seemed pained. I had to drag her
out from underneath the bed, and as I lifted her bulk onto
my lap, I noticed briefly how she had grown: her long legs
hung limply down, almost touching the floor. To gain her
confidence, I stroked her head. She did not purr as before.
Freddie stood by, holding the cup of medicine.

After quite a struggle, though half the brew spilled
down under her chin, matting the fur, we finally managed
to get some of it into her by using a tablespoonful at a time,
pushing the spoon between her clenched teeth at the side
of her jaws. Then I placed her gently in the dog basket
and covered her over with a blanket. Returning to the
campfire, I felt no need for food: my anxiety was choking
me.

There came a very strange sound from the hut. It
sounded like "Tok-a-tok, tok-a-tok." I hurried to the hut
with a storm lantern and found Gara-Yaka sitting on the

floor, cat-fashion, her neck outstretched as she vomited a deep yellow foamy substance. It seemed to come from deep down in her bowels. I suffered with her, and I know the drawn expression on her face could only have been matched by that on mine.

With wet newspapers I cleaned the mess and disinfected the patch, then burned the papers. Every hour, during the night, this vomiting continued. The vomiting, cleaning, and burning went on without a stop. Freddie kept the campfire going all night and assisted several times in dosing Gara-Yaka with herb tea. It all seemed endless, and I prayed for the dawn and the warmth of the sun. Finally they came, but by then my cheetah was so spent, she could barely stand.

Realizing that one or two more of these sessions would be the end of Gara-Yaka, I decided to administer some sort of nourishment. But what? Then I remembered that in my stores I had some concentrated meat extract. I handed a jar to Freddie and instructed him on its use. He brought a jug of lukewarm beef tea, and the task of force-feeding began. My cheetah refused to swallow, and the nourishing liquid oozed from the sides of her mouth, but we persevered and did succeed in getting a little down each time. But it was not long before it all came up again; so we fed and lost, fed and lost, every hour on the hour. And in between feeds we gave the fever-breaking brew. It seemed a losing battle.

By now the poor animal was in such great distress, what with continuous purging and vomiting, forced feeding, matted fur on chest and hindquarters, that I knew by her eyes she was pleading just to be left alone to die. But I refused to give up the fight for her life. I sponged her down with damp absorbent cotton and brushed out the knots in her fur.

After the grooming, she looked a little more comfortable. But I had to keep the hut door locked because she made several feeble attempts to get out, probably to go and die somewhere in the bush. I knew if she succeeded in getting out, I would not find her before it was too late.

By the third day and my third sleepless night, during which I had done nothing except nurse my cheetah, I noticed she was so weak that she was now absolutely mute. Her long legs buckled under her and she flopped down on her side. Her hip bones stuck out of her emaciated body. My pet seemed almost completely dehydrated. When will this end and how, I wondered. I resolved even more firmly that this sickness must be conquered, and we renewed our efforts—at the expense of her feeble wrath.

The strain of my fight against tremendous odds was beginning to tell on me. I had hardly eaten anything for those three days and nights. This was the beginning of the fourth day, with Freddie and Piet still standing solidly by. I wished I could have conveyed to Gara-Yaka their constant concern.

During the fourth night Gara-Yaka had a particularly severe attack and after it lay so still, with her now shriveled little head resting on my hand, that I really thought it was the end of a truly wonderful pal. My heart cried out at the futility of our combined efforts.

No! I would not let this be the end, so with hope and silent prayer I gave meat broth, this time with an eye-dropper. Could it be that she swallowed, though reluctantly? With breath held, I gave more and more. The doses were only a few drops at a time, but she was indeed swallowing as though the will to live had returned. I timed the periods of vomiting; they had become less frequent. I had to restrain myself lest I should be prematurely jubilant.

The fifth day came and I noticed a look of interest on Gara-Yaka's face when she saw the bowl and the dropper in my hand. She seemed to be waiting for the broth. Could it be or was I being overhopeful? I decided to test her condition by pouring the broth into a saucer and offering it to her. No one can imagine my relief when she actually lapped up the last drop of the life-giving broth!

I rushed out of the hut, which by now had the peculiar odor of sickness and near death about it. Freddie sat dejectedly by the fire, gazing at the leaping flames and probably wondering what to do next in an effort to help. I shouted in his language, "She has eaten!" His face lit up—flashing a white-toothed smile—for he also loved this cheetah pet of ours. Without any comment he set about preparing a feast.

Oh, yes! I ate that evening and so did Freddie and Piet. We laughed again and chatted about everything except Gara-Yaka. The nightmare was over and I slept a sleep drugged with happiness.

The sun rose the next morning in a golden glow of unsurpassed splendor, and I knew that all was well and that we could look forward to many more adventures with Gara-Yaka.

chapter 7

GARA-YAKA HAD her few chosen favorites among my friends. These she honored with a welcoming grunt and a prolonged sniffing, then a welcoming brush against the legs. But with all others she remained aloof, regarding them with a strangely cold look. For some reason she could not be friendly toward natives, except of course Freddie and Piet. When strangers came she would most times disappear into the bush, even missing meals; then when they had departed she would stroll out as though she had never been away.

By now she was past the ugly-duckling stage. With her high chassis and the small head on the end of her long neck, she reminded me of a swan. She walked with the carriage of a teen-age girl in her first pair of high-heeled shoes. But her sitting posture, dog-fashion, was very un-lady-like. Her puppy fat had gone and her fur had become smooth and fully spotted. The black spots seemed to stand out in relief against the coarser golden part of her pelt. Once while we were traveling in the Land Rover, I noticed that the wind picked out the black spots, so that they waved gently in the breeze. I examined the texture of the

Sitting in dog-fashion

spots and found them to be like soft, Persian-cat fur, while
the golden parts were more like dog's hair. Yet another
feature of the dog-cat make-up of a cheetah!

Gara-Yaka was born to chase—if not a ball, then a bird,
and if not that, it was her tail. One day she was very busy
chasing her tail, and she had almost caught it when Freddie
emerged from the bush: I saw him through the clouds of

dust she had raised. He was carrying a hessian sack which obviously contained something very much alive! I thought, "What on earth has the boy caught now?"

I soon found out. Two black crows! They were very young still, and Freddie said he had had no difficulty in catching them and popping them into the bag. They were easier to tame than any other bird or animal I had ever had.

Being unsure of their sex, I named them Mutt and Jeff. They became firm favorites of Gara-Yaka's, to the consternation of her already established pals, the pups. A favorite pastime of the crows was fetching and carrying twigs and then making a heap of them. The cheetah with her usual curiosity would sniff at the twigs and with a single sweep of her paw demolish the heap that had taken so long to build. Undaunted, Mutt and Jeff would start all over again.

The carnivorous crows shared Gara-Yaka's food, shamelessly stealing small juicy pieces of meat from under her nose, all the time voicing their sonorous "K'arrk, k'arrk," demanding more while still choking on the last chunk. After the meal they would hop all over the relaxing cheetah, pecking at her spots. She was very patient, and I wondered how long this would last. Then one day she lashed out with her paw at Mutt, who was brazenly pulling at the hairs in her ear. She struck him on the foot, and I tried everything to repair the damage, but he remained crippled. Yet this affliction neither hampered Mutt's agility nor did it deter him from seeking the cheetah's company. They remained good friends.

Mutt and Jeff were a thieving pair: all shiny objects such as knives, forks, spoons, cartridges, etc., had to be safely stowed away out of sight. They would carry these articles in their beaks and bury them in secret caches under bushes and trees. Nor did they know the difference be-

Mutt   *And Jeff*

tween clean laundry and soiled. They delighted in leaving their droppings on my freshly laundered shirts, or on my pillow and even on my tablecloth. This always proved an embarrassment when friends arrived unexpectedly. I had to hurry to inspect all the crows' favorite places before welcoming the guests.

At sunset the two crows would waddle, single file, into my bungalow and perch on the branch which we had fixed for them, to make them feel "at home." Come daybreak and they would start to imitate the yapping pups, waking all in the hut. Their repertoire consisted of Gara-Yaka's purr, her growl, and her meouw; the squeal of the pups, Rex's bark and the staccato "yap-yap" they loved using as an early morning alarm. Often I was not sure whether the sounds I heard were the real thing or just Mutt and Jeff proving their versatility.

We had a large white enamel basin which we kept filled with water and placed under a tree in the shade for Gara-Yaka and the dogs. But shortly after the advent of Mutt and Jeff this drinking place became a swimming pool. Squawks of joy came from the two crows as they romped and splashed in the water. The cheetah and the dogs lay, heads resting between forepaws, watching the performance and the fast disappearance of their water. Then the winged clowns would jump out onto the edge of the basin, make a few pecks into shiny blue-black feathers, and the comedy would really start. They would make long jumps with wings outstretched; like an airplane landing on a bumpy strip, they would touch down and fly, touch down and fly, till their feathers were free of all water.

The days were far too short for this pair of clowns who seemed to have so much to offer for the amusement of all present. They were a real asset. Perhaps one of their most amusing games was that of flapping their wings and hopping around Gara-Yaka to tell her they wanted to play. They hopped, skipped, and danced around the cheetah like cannibals around a cooking pot. Then the cheetah would open one eye wide and give a look which was meant to scare them off. But the warning had as much effect on Mutt and Jeff as the water they shook so expertly from their backs.

Often when Gara-Yaka had grown weary of the teasing crows she would gaze longingly into the surrounding bush. This was my cue to take her for a walk or on a trip of inspection. She was growing into a handsome cheetah with the first disheveled rufflets of mane showing.

On one of these trips I chose the top of a small "kop-

pie"—hillock—as my observation point. From this there was
an excellent view of the surrounding sparse bushland. We
rested in the shade for a while until she felt the urge to
expend some of her stored-up energy in fruitful chase of
beetles and butterflies and of imaginary prey—the latter in
the form of old tree stumps. I watched as she charged these
objects, her whiskers twitching and nostrils dilated. She
tumbled over her "catch" in a cartwheel and lay panting
with the sheer joy of living.

While Gara-Yaka was thus engaged, I looked around
casually, and on the opposite side of the koppie something stirred which attracted my attention.

I recognized a full-grown steenbuck ewe trying to appear unconcerned as she edged her way from the scrub.
The ewe's apparent casualness was very good play-acting
and would have put to shame many a movie star. Because
of it I paid more attention to her, and it was clear, in spite
of her efforts to deceive, that she was in fact very cautiously approaching a patch of long-stemmed red-top grass.

Revelation came. With a final careful scrutiny of the
surrounding bush, she appeared satisfied that the coast was
clear and that she was not being spoored. She then hurried
straight to the center of the patch of tasseled grass. There
rising from the grass was a small replica of the buck. Standing on its wobbly little legs it reached unmistakably for its
fountains of food.

An idyllic few minutes followed, during which the tiny
mouth sucked, nudged the source, sucked and nudged
again, gulping the nourishment eagerly. Meanwhile the
ewe stood with her head turned astern, caressing her fawn
with her muzzle and combing the silken little coat of her
offspring with her busy tongue. Yet another baby of the
bush was enjoying its bathing and feeding time.

An "ungh" from my cheetah brought my attention

back to her. She was hot from activity and was returning with open mouth and drooling tongue to share my shade. Almost instantly her attention was fixed on something. I followed the line of her interest and spotted a pair of saddle-back jackals coming into view from the sands of an ant-bear hole.

The jackals had apparently been sunning themselves together with their twin half-grown pups whom the mother had obviously been nursing, for the pups, not yet satiated, were clamoring for more. The parents, however, had more urgent business on their minds and, through some remarkable form of instruction, restrained the brood and made them remain obediently on the sand, while the older jackals began a cunning stalking of the suckling ewe and her fawn.

The steenbuck's alert motherly eyes had already seen the villains, and she reacted accordingly. She gave a final strong lick to her fawn which almost bowled it over and then determinedly sallied forth to the side of a bush directly in line with the approach of the parent jackals.

I must admit that I was already busy making calculations on how to rear the tender little orphaned fawn as the long-nosed, bewhiskered villains made for the defenseless mother.

I had seldom seen jackals in action on their own behalf to procure a meal. Even now it was probably only because they were out to show some of the finer points of hunting to their pups. These not unattractive-looking animals are usually the chief lackeys of the great carnivores to whom they pay royal homage for being permitted to pick up leftovers. If the scraps prove insufficient, they prey largely on small mammals and game birds and their eggs. Nor do they consider it below their dignity to vary their menu with some juicy insects and fruits in season.

Gara-Yaka intently watched the developments as though she herself had been instructed by a tutor to learn from these foxy parents. I did notice that now and then she cast a look of interest at the small steenbuck standing stiffly on guard against the oncoming foe.

It is written in the Word that the Lord tempers the wind to the shorn lamb, and that a mother is a tower of strength when it comes to defending her young. Apparently the parent jackals were unaware of this, and they crept up together to frighten the ewe off. The defending mother dug her heels securely into the ground and bent her forelegs slightly like a bull ready to gore a victim. The jackals might just as well have tried to frighten off the Statue of Liberty for all the result they achieved!

Now they changed their tactics and made short foxy rushes. This triggered off an avalanche. The ewe charged them! Like whipped dogs, the two retreated, jabbering insults at the courageous mother. I chuckled inwardly.

My rejoicings were a little previous though, for the jackals returned to the ring, undaunted. They tried an encircling maneuver but with exactly the same results. Now I blushed for them, because I think I know how they must have felt. The steenbuck, with her head lowered and her eyes wild, made a sudden rush at the male and stampeded him right out of the picture.

The scene now became a mothers' duel. The female jackal was determined to regain some dignity, however slight. She slithered closer to the plucky little steenbuck who now, undoubtedly, held all the trump cards. The buck made a swift and furious charge at the persistent enemy and butted her so hard that I heard the thud of the impact and the recipient's bark of pain. The mother jackal, too, now went off the scene with tail dragging on the ground.

At this point Gara-Yaka stood up, but not to applaud. She had developed an interest in the jackal pups, probably thinking they would play with her as our own pups did. She crept a short distance toward the jackal babies and then started a stalking game. But she was soon spotted and the little ones knew instinctively what best to do. They bolted for the ant-bear hole and practically fell in. Gara-Yaka loped up to the loose sand and sniffed around the place where the pups had lain. She lifted her head and made the characteristic feline grimace while indexing the new scent and doubtlessly deploring the pups' unsporting attitude.

I was about to recall her when a great ballyhoo broke the silence. The parent jackals had slunk back to explain their defeat to the young ones, when they found their sandy hearth under foreign occupation. All their bitterness was now expressed in howling, barking, and jibbering, while they hopped around in true Southern barn-dance fashion, protesting the invasion of their property.

Hardly did Gara-Yaka and I realize that all the noises they made were actually calls for help, when there came from the bushes, from the grass, and from the glades reinforcements in swift response to the urgent appeal. I counted nine additional jackals, all of whom made such a fearful din barking, howling, and dancing around that Gara-Yaka thought it wise to sit up and take notice.

It amazed me to see the bold front put up by the pack after the poor show I had witnessed only a short while earlier. In pairs and in groups they rushed Gara-Yaka, their fangs bared and their bushy tails fanned out thick and held erect like those of squabbling dogs.

My cheetah had indeed stirred up a hornet's nest! She looked totally bewildered at this unexpected turn of events. All she had wanted was a game with the pups. She backed away from the sand a few feet at a time edging her way toward me. Then, determined to keep the cheetah name unbesmirched and perhaps also to show me her mettle, Gara-Yaka seemed to pull up her spotted socks as she rushed at the three jackals that had ventured rather close to her.

She, too, bared her almost mature teeth and growled like a leopard, then charged at the three musketeers while whirling her tail in a great circle to keep course. Her zigzag, arch-backed, spring-powered sprint sent her into the midst of the jackals and they scattered like chaff in a whirlwind. Then she bounded back in rocking-horse cheetah gait, bearing the unmistakable smile of glory on her face. I could not restrain myself from planting a kiss of pride on her furry forehead.

Gara-Yaka's attack had knocked the wind out of the jackal relief force. Though they all scattered, they did not disperse and kept trying to lure us away from the vicinity of the ant-bear hole where their young nephews were in hiding. Those two worthies, however, now sensing their chance, slipped from the hole and sped to their agonized kinfolk, much to the latter's relief and joyous yapping.

Later in the falling dusk we made our way home. The C-shaped moon was rising and we could still hear the jackal clan howling their long drawn-out cry—so character-istic a sound of the African bush—dogging us from their hunting grounds. I think we both felt that we had made harmless but unforgiving enemies.

Before we left, I noted with satisfaction that the plucky little steenbuck had returned once more to her hidden fawn and, tossing the tiny creature vigorously with her head, induced it to leave the place for a safer hide-out under a thick thorn bush.

chapter 8

I ENCOURAGED MY cheetah to play with her ball as often as she was inclined. I threw, kicked, and bounced the ball to help her practice the chase: the ball simulated the flight of wild animals.

A cheetah mother would probably have trained her cubs to hunt and kill by similar practice. The hunt begins with that patient and spellbinding forward-slithering stalk, in which cheetahs excel. Lions rush and leap, and the killing bite is usually within a few yards of where the victim has last been. With the cheetah, the stalking is followed by a deadly race to catch up with the fleeing animal. After a sudden swift rush, the cheetah runs alongside its prey, following level with the quarry, keeping up with its every evasive move, and then knocks it out of its stride and kills it with a locked stranglehold on the throat.

I wondered how much of this I could teach Gara-Yaka and how much of it would come naturally—I worried the way a mother does when her child first goes to school. But I need not have been concerned.

"Bring the ball!" I said in a firm voice. She had known these words ever since she had been given a tennis ball by

my pal, Cyril, the young Police Inspector, who was affectionately referred to as Gara-Yaka's uncle. By watching
Rex retrieve the ball, the cheetah soon learned the art.

Obediently Gara-Yaka brought the ball. She held it in
her mouth with something like a smile on her lips, her eyes
sparkling. Sometimes she placed the ball down at my feet,
but often she locked her jaws on it, so that it was impos-
sible to take it away from her. The dogs were permitted to
scramble after it, but in an instant she would scoop it up
and bolt before the dogs could get a hold on it.

But she did not always have the game her own way. On
occasion the dogs resented her manner, and when she
brought the ball to me they would nip her hard on the hind
legs. At this she would drop the ball and, with ears flattened, she would snarl and then snap at the teasing culprits, whereupon the dogs scattered, for her teeth were
sharper than theirs and her half-playful nips really hurt.

At other times she allowed the dogs to harass her while
she proudly brought the ball, touching it down at my feet
like a scoring rugby-forward. Then after a beautiful backward leap and some back-pedaling, she would wait, one
foreleg raised, expectantly, for the next throw.

Her skill in catching the ball gave me a great measure
of satisfaction. If the call of the wild came and she decided
to leave me, she could at least exist on francolin, rabbit,
and guinea-fowl until she had learned the more difficult
art of pulling down antelope.

She well understood it was feeding time when I said
"kitchen" and tinkled the saucer with a teaspoon. Her
fondness for dog biscuits had now become habit, and she
could always be tempted to come if I said the word "biscuits." And she may well have been the only chocolate-
eating cheetah in the world; her liking for it bordered on
passion: it quite equaled her desire for a succulent bird.

Sweet-toothed Gara-Yaka

Gara-Yaka took regular baths in the loose powdery sand under the Mopani and wallowed luxuriously, rolling on her back, all four legs up. After this she would sit dog-like, while performing her ablutions with the royal dignity of a Siamese cat. Again I say Nature created a curious blend of canine and feline in the cheetah.

In her robust joi de vivre she sometimes overreached herself in her boisterous play with the pups, and rolled them over with too great gusto or hammered them in a rough-and-tumble manner with her long slender front legs. But when I shouted "Inside!" or "Outside!" depending on whether the rowdiness occurred within or without the hut, she always went, looking chastised.

Before Gara-Yaka was mature enough to look after herself, I found her sniffing at the closed door or contemplating a jump through the open window at night when the bush was alive with sounds. To stop her restlessness I ordered her to "Get into the basket!" She always obeyed. Her only acknowledgment of my firm commands was a short sharp mew, her way of shouting back at me.

Soft cajoling words always achieved far more with her than loud, angry commands. Her reaction to the latter was a flattening of ears and spitting and growling with teeth bared. She was no lackey to do everyone's bidding!

She could be jealous, too, and showed it: from mild nuzzling away of my hand when I fondled the dogs, to an open snarl and a cuff on the ear to those who had not shied away at her warning scowl. That scowl was a sullen glare which changed her mild look to an aggressively ferocious one.

But she loved Rex and the pups in her own way, and in fact she once nearly gave her life to save Rex.

That was on an oppressive evening. The sky was laden with gray thunder clouds edged with flame-lily shades as the sun set in a purple shroud. My trackers were pulling into position dry stumps of trees for our campfire. The trees had long since been uprooted by elephant, and the bush was littered with crumbly firewood. At sunset the bush immediately cooled, so Gara-Yaka and the three dogs occupied their usual places around the fire. The flames grew warm and Freddie set out my camp chair and a drink on a stool.

The campfire always had a hypnotic effect on my cheetah: the comforting warmth seemed to knock her semiconscious. She would lie on her back, long hind legs outstretched, forelegs pulled up to either side of her face. A sound unimportant to the pups and to the drowsy Gara-Yaka sent Rex quietly downwind to investigate.

What happened then was so quick that my eye could hardly follow the event. A blurred black and gold mass streaked from the bush and fell on the sniffing, half-suspecting Rex. The throaty snarl of a large leopard mingled with the agonized yelp of the dog. There was a momentary flurry of bodies, striking claws, and gnashing teeth. Then the leopard was taking Rex away.

At the leopard's first snarl, Gara-Yaka was on her feet growling, watching the uneven fight. Fleetingly, I noticed she was contemplating an attack. As the leopard retreated, dragging Rex into the bush, Gara-Yaka rushed at it and leaped on its back, biting deep into the huge cat's neck, shaking it, and finally forcing it to release the dog. The surprised leopard turned, rolled over, and dislodged the cheetah. In a split second it was on top of Gara-Yaka.

There followed a short but sharp and amazing fight. The cheetah kicked with her long hind legs for all she was worth, and when her stiff claws found a hold here and there, she raked away the heavy marauder, preventing it from inflicting serious injuries.

I whipped off my hat and, followed by the furiously barking pups, rushed at the leopard and beat it with the hat while the pups fastened their teeth into its hind legs and tail. The leopard would surely have turned on us had not Freddie and Piet joined in the melee, hurling burning sticks and shouting loudly. This was too much for the leopard: it side-leaped, giving one of the pups a fare-well clout as it flew into the bush. The pup rolled along the ground yelping murder, though it was unhurt.

Poor Rex was still alive, but so badly clawed and bitten

that I knew she would not survive the night. I attended to her terrible wounds, bandaged her up as best I could, and gave her a spoonful of anti-shock mixture. We all sat with her, trying to comfort her.

I could tell by Gara-Yaka's restlessness that the leopard had not gone far. Like a thief it was lurking around the camp probably hoping to strike again. Freddie and Piet told me they thought it to be a large male, old and extremely cunning, a clever hunter. His speed had lessened with the passing years, and now he generally lay on branches over game-trails so that he could drop on the unwary as they passed.

Leopards are inordinately fond of dog flesh and will go far out of their way to obtain it, but nevertheless, hunting must have been completely unrewarding if the old boy was willing to attack a dog in a camp which had a fire blazing. Any other leopard would have avoided such action like the plague.

Gara-Yaka remained in a tense condition after the fight, and would not permit me to attend to the bloody gashes on her neck and her chest; she licked the wounds she could reach. It was quite apparent that the encounter had upset her and put her into a very aggressive mood. She was ready to flare up and fight.

The pups were still trembling with excitement and sniffed at the dressings on Rex. Finally I had to lock them up in the storeroom for the night—for their own safety and to prevent them from bothering Rex. But at the first gray of dawn I saw Rex was sinking fast. Placing one hand under her faithful head, I stroked her with the other. She gave a deep sigh and was gone.

At sunrise we buried her in the bush she knew and loved so well, and covered the spot with flat rocks to prevent jackals and hyenas from disturbing her remains.

The leopard's spoor had been partly obliterated by a strong breeze, but where it was visible it showed pugmarks as big as those of an almost mature lion. We tracked him for quite a distance southward, but lost the trail on the stony ground along the banks of the waterless Majali River. His lair must have been somewhere there or in the rocky hills a few miles farther south by the Limpopo River.

Gara-Yaka found the leopard spoor for us several times, but finally lost it, and we noticed she was far more interested in a fresh lion spoor which she was now following eagerly. The spoors were those of a family of lions with two half-grown cubs. I knew this family. It was the pride whose impala-hunting Gara-Yaka had interrupted some time before, when she was chasing her first buck. So this was the family's home ground: we were in their own backyard. When my cheetah lifted her nose off the ground I could see she was very ill at ease. With her hackles up, she sniffed the air deeply. I knew the lions to be very near, probably watching us.

Suddenly Gara-Yaka picked up the scent. She gave a trembling growl. Like a weathercock, she turned her head into the shifting wind. I followed her gaze, and there, watching us, was a big black-maned lion partly obscured by a clump of dry grass. He was not more than 30 yards away. His eyes drifted idly from us to the cheetah and back again, at a loss to reconcile the association. These large males are incredibly lazy, and, unless disturbed, they dodge all issue. I tried to look casually away to indicate my disinterest in him, but somehow our eyes locked; there was momentarily a glint of mean yellow in his, and then, to my relief, he yawned as though very bored, got up leisurely, and went to lie down further up on the mound.

I had to pet and reassure Gara-Yaka, for she feared the

lions more than we did. (Lions are not naturally man-eaters, so at least we were safe on that score.) But Gara-Yaka's apprehension began to worry me, especially as the females and the cubs were not in sight. Fortunately, we did not have to wait long to find out where they were. We did not see the lionesses expertly stalking us, but we did see the two clumsy cubs slowly belly-creeping up on us. At times young lions are stupid. The inquisitive females and the cubs were apparently trying to get a closer look at us and the cheetah. They could not have been hungry, for I could see the remnants of their kill, a wildebeest, near where the old boy had been; in the heat, the stench was overpowering, and the carcass was infested with buzzing bluebottles.

As a rule lions jealously guard their kill, and I wondered if these thought we had come to rob them. But I realized that this was not the case, for if so they would have attacked as soon as they were aware of our presence.

It became increasingly clear that the cubs were out for fun—at our expense. A lion's attention is magnetically drawn to all moving things, just as is a cheetah's. Consequently, I had to prevent Gara-Yaka from making a break for it. Such action would have flushed the whole pride with unpredictable results.

I whispered to Freddie and Piet to arm themselves with stones; then I bent over to grasp Gara-Yaka by the loose skin on the back of her neck. Both trackers now pelted the approaching cubs with stones. With hollow grunts both retired, thoroughly ashamed at having been discovered. I had a very difficult task holding the cheetah against her will and the natural instinct which prompted quick departure. She had apparently not forgotten her skirmish with one of these cubs.

It was a near thing! A vulture saved our face and the

An aristocrat of the bushland

Piet and Freddie with the eight-foot, one-inch coat of Rex's killer

situation for all. Out of nowhere, or perhaps we had just not noticed it in our anxiety, it sailed down and settled near the kill. That was enough for the old male to become rampant, and with a great growl he took several swipes at the frightened scavenger. The lion's growl is a fearsome sound: a deep-chested rumble that shakes the earth, or so it seems when one is close by. The roar brought the lionesses out of their hiding to defend their larder.

The vulture had speedily retreated to a very high tree and from there looked down enviously at a tiny long-eared fox and a pair of jackals whom these lions permitted to feed on their stinking kill. I have seen these small courtiers of the King of Beasts jostle their lords with impunity for a tasty morsel. Once in a while they pay with their lives if the lord is surly.

As much as these lions suffered the fox and the jackals to pilfer their kill, they hated the vulture and loathed the thieving hyena. Just then one of the jackals whined at full blast and was joined immediately by the other. They had spotted the hyena that had quietly crept up in the hope of picking up morsels from the royal table. Warned of the thief by the jackals, one of the lionesses rushed at the hyena which was sidling out from cover. She slashed out at it with a forepaw, and it fled as it uttered its maniacal cackle.

The jackals followed the hyena, escorting it from the premises. How the jackals howled and how provokingly the hyena laughed. While all leonine eyes were concentrated on this maneuver, it was our chance to leave. We made our exit at a leisurely pace, so as not to arouse undue interest, but our hearts were beating fast. By the time the jackals returned to resume their interrupted meal, we were safely away.

chapter 9

AFTER A FEW days I paid a visit to the rocky koppies some 15 miles south by the Limpopo. These koppies were high outcrops with flat tops, resembling aircraft carriers. On them, from about the tenth century A.D. to some 300 years ago, caucasoid-type Hottentot chiefs lived as ruling lords of the rock fortresses. Against invading Bantu from the north they had built ramparts and generally reinforced the sheer, practically impassable walls.

In the lush valleys among the rock forts, where dense forests of large trees are festooned with beautiful creepers, there stand magnificent River Palms. Here large cattle herds grazed in those days. Archaeological excavations have revealed ash middens and bone heaps 20 feet high in some places, while on the flat tops of the rock islands have been found the chief's burial places with gold beads and images carved from solid gold, and weapons and remains of sacrificed cattle of ancient pre-Bantu days.

Now the indigenous Bushman, the oldest inhabitant of Africa, and the Hottentot have disappeared from these parts, leaving behind their mysterious paintings, their smelting furnaces, stone habitats, and traces of ancient

religious cults in inexplicable graves. Vultures sail the
clear blue of the sky and the majestic silence is only broken
by the loud cry "Wahu" of the sentry baboon high up on
a towering cliff, warning the troop, foraging below, to
beware.

At our appearance the baboons scattered. Instinctively,
Gara-Yaka gave chase, caught one of the scrambling creatures, and held it loosely by the neck. The captive screamed
blue murder; the sound echoing through the valley was
beyond description. But it brought answering barks from
the wooded folds of a ravine where a troop had taken
refuge. One by one, dog-faced baboons peered at us
through the tree branches. They seemed to be every-
where: on ledges, on jutting crags of rock. A growing
chorus of sympathetic bellows, barks, and shrieks rent the
air.

Their own re-echoing noises, it seemed, had given some
form of encouragement to the baboons, for they began
descending from their trees and from the rock face and
mustering into a rough military phalanx. The ranks grew
to scores in no time and then advanced on Gara-Yaka.

Shoulder to shoulder in a half-moon formation, the
baboons barked a dire threat at my cheetah. The battle
line was inching slowly forward when Gara-Yaka stood up,
still holding the screaming quarry, but looking uneasy. I
called her, and at the familiar sound of her name, she
released the hysterical baboon and with a commendable
backward leap sped toward us, having no doubt realized
the weight of the frightful odds against her.

Like unleashed flood waters the baboon horde now
poured forth around their rescued kin, and then they withdrew, assisting the lucky one back to their rocky hide-out.
I had feared the worst: that they might attack us.

The roused baboon is no mean adversary. A full-grown

Baboons' castle

male has canine fangs longer than those of a leopard, and he can use them with devastating efficiency. Because of this he is treated with respect even by lions and leopards whose diet often consists of baboon. A baboon's enormous teeth can easily disembowel a dog, or for that matter an inexperienced cheetah like Gara-Yaka, in a matter of seconds. In a fight the baboon first bites, then pushes away the victim with all his hands, and repeats the performance again and again, until the victim is literally ripped to shreds.

Though I have seen lone baboons in kudu and impala company, they live mostly with their fellows in troops, greedy, quarrelsome, and almost friendless. They seldom choose hunting grounds in flat bush country, preferring steep cliffs and inaccessible rock ledges where their amazing skill as climbers comes to the fore. They live in caves and fissures, knowing well that huddled up in these dormitories they are completely safe from the predators of the night.

Looking up I noticed that some of them were now climbing along the cliff ledges in pursuit of vultures. I stopped to watch what would follow, for part of the purpose of my visit here was to tag with a ring some of the new fledgling vultures for an ornithologist friend. I hoped that the baboons would betray the position of the nests in the fissures on the cliff face.

At the base of the sheer cliffs I found the remains of a few vultures, mainly adult birds—some freshly killed, others old. In each case they were torn to pieces with their flesh stripped off. Gara-Yaka sniffed at the ragged remains and turned her head away with a grimace of disgust, sharing the leonine antipathy for vultures.

Suddenly Gara-Yaka bounced up like a ball, whistled, and threw herself backward in fright. Something had landed between us. It was the hideous bald head and part of the scrawny neck of a decapitated vulture. I glanced up and saw a baboon on a ledge tearing at a large bird, scattering feathers, and ravenously devouring flesh.

Gara-Yaka could not be persuaded to accompany us on the climb up the rock outcrop. She came a little way, looked down, and became terrified of the height. I had to do the job I had undertaken, so we took her back to the Land Rover and left her in Piet's care. Freddie came back with me carrying the rifle.

To the uninitiated, ringing baby vultures—while the parent birds, with wing spans of up to seven feet, hover overhead—may appear a hazardous operation. But it is dangerous only so far as the climbing is concerned. Surprisingly, considering its size, the vulture is exceptionally cowardly.

Still, at first I did feel a little unsure when I climbed out onto a steep ledge where two of these large birds sat in a cradle of twigs. The sitters were white-backed vultures, the most common in this area. They were so dark brown in parts that they looked dirty, but their lighter parts appeared immaculate in contrast. The vulture heads were cocked to one side and the long snake-like necks were outstretched to their full length. Cold eyes surveyed me icily. I stepped down to where the birds sat. As the nearest one refused to budge, I gave it a gentle but firm push with the toe of my boot. I was prepared for a hard peck in retaliation, but instead, it toppled off the ledge and fell quite a few feet, apparently petrified, before it opened its great wings and soared beautifully into the distance. The remaining vulture sat motionless.

There was a fledgling in the nest and to be able to ring it I unceremoniously shoved the parent bird aside. It withdrew into the farthest corner and cowered there, leaving the infant to its fate.

Ringing is done annually to study these birds' migratory habits, which are still a mystery. It is known that vultures roam hundreds of miles from their birthplace, and at least one mid-Transvaal bird was caught for identification in Southern Rhodesia, 500 miles away.

It was no easy job to find nests. Here and there it became necessary to be lowered by rope to reach a well-concealed nursery. Finally when we had traversed the whole of the spacious rock island and were descending on the far side, we came upon a tangled growth of creepers and rock scrub, some 50 feet up from the base of the rock face.

"Sir! Leopard down there," Freddie whispered, choking with the urgency of his words. Sure enough, some 200 yards away there lay "Spots," sunning itself on a jutting flat rock slab. I decided to get a closer view of this magnificent specimen. We were passing the tangled growth of creepers and were stopped by the overpowering stench of decaying meat. Somewhere in that tangle was the home of the leopard, its rotting kill reeking to high heaven. Freddie and I grimaced, holding our breath.

Without warning there was a rustle above us and a second leopard appeared. It charged. Often in an emergency, one's movements and reactions are inexplicable. Some form of mental mechanism sets one's senses and muscles into action. Freddie shoved the rifle into my hands.

We saw the beast coming from a ledge some 30 feet up. It was charging downhill with the speed of a falling boulder. I took quick aim over the open-sighted .375 Magnum and fired. It was almost a point-blank shot. The leopard shuddered at the impact of the 270-grain soft-nosed bullet, flopped inertly, and tumbled in a heap between the crouching Freddie and me. I did not even know where I had hit it. "Ow!" Freddie exclaimed. "A very close shave," I muttered and wiped my forehead with the back of my hand. Freddie's eyes were like saucers in his ashen face. He never did say what my color was. Just then the leopard jerked.

The tracker looked down at the heavy animal in shocked silence and, in spite of his dazed condition, he seemed ready to take off. The heavy clawed paws jerked again in a spasm. I pushed the rifle muzzle into the grinning mouth, ready to fire again if the leopard showed signs of life— but it was quite dead. "This one killed Rex, sir," Freddie said after a time. He stabbed a horny thumb at the leopard's belly, pointing out unhealed claw rakings where Gara-Yaka had scraped the marauder. I looked to where the other leopard had been, but it was gone. It was probably this one's mate.

I kept a lookout while Freddie took off the leopard's coat, for leopards are sentimental creatures and the other might have decided to dispute our business. I could not help wondering at the strange coincidence which had brought us to the killer's lair.

The pelt of our attacker was an unusually large one, measuring eight feet and one inch, a good foot longer than the average. I guessed the weight of the animal to be about 135 pounds; it was certainly the biggest leopard I had come across.

Piet had heard the shot and realized we were having a "spot of trouble." He saw the other leopard running down the hill. At first Gara-Yaka growled at the folded pelt, but gradually she warmed toward it, and by the time we drove down to the river to check the early winter water level, she was rubbing her face against it and going into convulsions, rolling over it in an expression of excitement.

I coaxed her away from the skin and took her down to the river to drink near the spot where, a year ago, her dam had come to such an untimely end.

Several weeks later when we were visiting this area again, we flushed a water-buck at the water's edge and it ran into the now very low river splashing over the shallows.

It is said at campfires that this species of buck takes refuge in water against predators who dare not follow it there for fear of crocodiles, and that the reptile not only does not harm the buck but actually protects it. It is difficult to take sides on such issues. Seldom is it the eyewitness who relates the story, but rather one who has heard it second- or third- or fourth-hand.

I will say, though, that the first part of that story is true, because on seeing Gara-Yaka the water-buck took flight into the water, instead of escaping on dry land. But as for the second part, well this might have been an occasion that was an exception to the rule. In any event a crocodile— and not a large one—broke surface next to where the water-buck was standing, and with a powerful sweep of its tail knocked the buck off its feet. With lightning speed, it grabbed the victim by its muzzle and held it under water to drown.

The luckless buck kicked and threw itself about in a desperate attempt to obtain release, but to no avail. Its movements lessened and gradually ceased altogether. Not far downstream in a deeper pool another monster broke surface. This one I knew by its great size. It was old friend Mulembe, the sacred crocodile.

Mulembe lifted his huge hideous head well above the water and with neck arched surveyed the scene, listening. His jagged tail, too, lay in a series of long arches along the surface of the water. Having ascertained what he sought, he took off upstream like a mighty torpedo.

The smaller reptile was busy dragging the dead buck into deeper water—perhaps to its lair—when Mulembe arrived. Suddenly the water boiled as Mulembe attacked, both crocodiles fighting desperately for possession of the kill. But the larger creature did not succeed with the first rush, as he probably had hoped. He now lay by and began a war of nerves, opening wide those terrible jaws, clamping them shut again and again, with a sound like that of hitting water with a heavy plank. A more impressive demonstration of spiteful bullying would have been difficult to perform.

But even in reptile society possession is nine-tenths of the law. The smaller crocodile was undaunted by the cold war and obviously not prepared to give up its property without a fight. Mulembe drew away as though to flee, and this brought the younger one on boldly. The wily giant then made a sudden turn enabling him to seize the other in the flank with the intent of rendering it powerless.

The smaller one was agile and a great battler, but Mulembe was a crafty veteran with many years' experience. The plucky little one never really had a chance. Squeezed at its middle, its forequarters rose out of the water and its jaws opened in the manner of a howling jackal. There came from its throat a yell and a long gurgle of hellish hideousness. The battle was over, and Mulembe took possession of the prize.

From the beginning to the sad end of the episode, Gara-Yaka watched with hackles up and lashing tail, indicating her instinctive displeasure at the sight of her most detested enemies.

chapter 10

WHEN MULEMBE towed away the prize, Gara-Yaka broke into a purr dotted with a series of whines, as chained dogs do when wanting to pursue a cat or some other quarry. She talked by purring—to show her excitement, her joy and contentment, or simply the unbounded energy which had to have expression.

My cheetah had grown into a slinky beauty standing just over two feet at the shoulders. I had become deeply attached to her, and the thought that one day she would choose to return to her natural environs filled me with foreboding. How soon this might happen I dared not guess, but undoubtedly the time must come for our positions to be reversed: now I still owned Gara-Yaka, but someday she would own me because I could never forget her.

The secret fear of losing my cheetah to her rightful surroundings gave birth to a dream of creating my own wilderness, like the Kruger Park or the Gorongoza Reserve, where she and all wild animals could roam free without fear of poachers or trophy hunters. As time passed this dream became almost an obsession. My mind was filled with plans to ensure the safety of my cheetah and the preservation of all other wild life.

A little over 300 years ago, Barretto de Rezende, a Portuguese official, arrived in the land between the Zambezi and the Limpopo Rivers to make a report to the king of Portugal on his African possessions. Señor Rezende traveled inland at a season when the summer floods were subsiding, and as the waters withdrew to the river course, the amazed official saw the land stocked with elephant, buffalo, wildebeest, eland, kudu, and water-buck in such great numbers that, according to his report, in certain pastures as many as 6,000 animals grazed together.

Such was the picture before the days of telescopic rifles and hunting safaris. Now there are few places left in Africa where one may see the like of this. Today there are only remnants of those once great herds, and a century hence men may wonder how a herd of live wild animals looked. For the advance of civilization drives away game, destroys the wonderful natural heritage. And, once extinct, wild life can never again be re-created. I see no reason why future generations should not have the right to see the graceful leap of an impala, witness the amazing strength and capacity of an elephant, hear the mournful cry of the hyena or the roar of a lion as dawn breaks; why should they not also delight in the gaudy plumage of a red-breasted lurie or laugh at the hoarse cry and clowning of a hornbill?

The area I had in mind for my preserve was a typical Mopani bushland, which produces palatable sour grass on which the game wax fat in the spring and in the early summer. There were a few pans—small lakes—and also numerous deep pools and water holes in the otherwise dry river beds. Here in this comparatively small portion of land I dreamed of my own controlled wilderness. But I

Having a good laugh

realized that my hopes were far beyond my means, for to purchase those lands would cost many thousands.

In many respects Gara-Yaka now behaved like a mixture of leopard and wolf dog. It fascinated me to watch her slink along the game trail with the litheness of a leopard and then change to the easy gait of a wolf dog. Here and there she made a spurt and was quickly out of sight, pursuing some scent she had picked up.

Her compressed body and narrow fragile-looking chest was built for speed; on her dainty feet she had hard pads like those of a dog and with her unsheathed claws she could take a firm hold on the ground to propel her at lightning speed. She used her long stiffly stretched tail as a rudder which enabled her to achieve feints by turning quickly at amazing angles when speeding. After a burst of speed she would brake herself and lie down panting, drooling saliva, her pink tongue like an upturned spoon.

On the hunt as at home, Gara-Yaka was a practical joker. Often she would speed off on the pretext of following a scent, and then she would make a mock attack from behind a bush or dart up a leaning tree trunk and wait, hidden among the branches until we arrived, so that she could drop on us like a leopard.

After these playful attacks, Gara-Yaka's black lines of "tear stains" appeared to be drawn into a grin. No doubt she best enjoyed the game when she succeeded in surprising us.

It was during one of our two-week-long patrols that Gara-Yaka threw up her shiny nose and sniffed hard. She looked at me as if to say, "Watch this!" and she was off. After a time she returned dragging something large and queer. At first we could not recognize her trophy although it had the shape of a buck.

Before she dropped it at our feet we saw that it was the stripped skeleton of an impala. The bones still had lots of meat fragments left; someone had used a knife hastily to strip for biltong. The meat on the carcass was already a little high, but by no means putrid. Bluebottle flies followed the carcass, flying around and around in their grim dance macabre.

Gara-Yaka darted up the path again in the direction from which she had brought the skeleton, came back to rub against my legs and mewed, then dashed off again, purring very loudly, only to return again and mew. I knew this meant that she wished us to follow her. We did.

Not more than 150 yards on, in a timbered thicket, we found the skeletons of nine more impala: females

and young rams with immature horns. It was easy to tell
from the signs that the poachers who had been in action
here were in a great hurry. All the meat had been stripped
off the hindquarters, the two long fillets on either side of
the spine had been taken, as had some of the meat from
the lower neck and shoulders. But the other parts, un-
suitable for biltong, had been left on the carcasses.

It was an unpleasant shock to realize that poachers
were operating so far within my area. Not that any game-
studded land was ever free from them, but this lot was
obviously a greedy bunch who callously shot every moving
thing, including ewes in calf.

The spiced and salted biltong strips can only be left
wrapped in the skin of the animal for 24 hours, after which
period they must be hung in a breeze to dry out. I suspected
that the poachers had a camp somewhere for that purpose,
unless they slipped over the border to the safety of adjoining territories.

Car-tire tracks remain visible a long while in the bush.
With biltong from ten impala—some 300 pounds on the
truck—the tracks must show up even more prominently
and the weight would certainly slow down the progress
of the light type of vehicle suitable for bush travel. The
game carcasses were barely a day old, so the culprits could
not have gone far.

Piet reported having found the tracks of a light vehicle.
We got down to examine the direction it had taken.
Sand particles falling from moving wheels usually form
a wedge indicating the vehicle's direction. In this instance
it pointed east. I might have guessed this, for a circle of
vultures filled the sky there.

Gara-Yaka was very excited. She squeaked, uttered her
"Unghs," and purred all in turn. With tail erect she
sniffed the ground, and I was sure her nose had told her

the story of what had taken place here. She took her place
beside me in the Land Rover; Freddie and Piet sat on the
hood, resting their feet on the front bumper to watch the
tracks and to guide me.

A car drive in the bush is no smooth hayride. We call
it bush-crashing. The undefined trail winds and turns,
ascends and descends, generally following a shaky rhap-
sodical course. Bushes and branches hammer on the sides
and on the windows. From pebbly and sandy dunes the
path nosedives into steep-walled dongas littered with sharp
rocks. To climb out of these dry watercourses is quite as
difficult as to descend into them. The car travels like a ship
on rough seas—bouncing, lurching, straining—and gets
completely out of hand in sandy patches.

Soon we came upon a stretch of open grassland with scattered scrub and trees. This was the place above which the
vultures were circling. We left the car and Gara-Yaka led
us straight to a spot where four half-stripped carcasses lay.
Our arrival drove away a small pack of piebald wild hunting dogs. I had wondered what had kept the vultures circling in the air, for these flying refuse bins of the wilds
usually settle as near the kill as circumstances permit, but
now it was obvious that the vicious hunting dogs were
responsible. These large-eared savage brothers of our
domesticated dogs are merciless in their punishment of any
living creature who interferes with their prey: once we
came upon a lioness they had killed; either she had tried
to share their kill or, more likely, they had taken hers.

The dogs had chewed off much of the meat left by the
biltong hunters and had eaten into the ribs and finer bones.
The carcasses were of two impala, a young kudu cow, and
a wildebeest. I took hold of Gara-Yaka to prevent her from
going after the wild dogs. She would not have stood a
chance had they chosen to attack her.

Freddie and Piet were examining a track close under a bush when Freddie cried out and jumped back. From the end of one of his fingers dangled a snake, hooked on by its fangs. My shocked and terrified tracker was trying to shake off the reptile by swinging his arm wildly like a whip.

The snake hung on grimly for a few seconds before it was dislodged and plopped on the ground. Piet speedily disposed of it. It was a young puff adder. Freddie immediately came to show me the fang-punctured finger. We applied ligatures, one on the finger and the others above the wrist and the elbow. I always carried an anti-snake-bite kit in the Land Rover, so we were able to give Freddie the prescribed treatment. But I had not renewed the serum for some time and was concerned lest it should be ineffective. I sucked at the bitten finger, drawing as hard as I could to rid the poor boy of the poisonous liquid.

To continue on the trail of the poachers now was quite out of the question. Freddie had to be attended to in camp or the results might be fatal. Already he had very sharp pains in his finger. Gara-Yaka had to sit on the back seat, but she went willingly, sensing the gravity of the situation. She purred loudly and treated Freddie to prolonged raspy licks on his neck and ears. Within 20 minutes Freddie complained that the pain was traveling up his right arm, which showed distinct swelling. I drove homeward as fast as possible.

The symptoms were becoming progressively worse. Around the bite the finger started to discolor. Freddie now complained of severe headache, giddiness, and burning eyes. A few minutes later he was barely able to speak: the paralysis of the throat had started.

I stopped the car and felt for his pulse; the beats were too fast and too strong. His face was distorted by the pain flooding his chest. I gave him a second injection high in the left hip, hoping that this would provide some relief.

I knew I could do no more. It was now up to Freddie's resistance and the will of the Great Mudimu, Patron of Brush-hunters, to fight the battle. This live-or-die period was hard to bear. Although I knew my tracker had a strong constitution I nevertheless prayed to the Great Mudimu to consider benevolently our appeal.

Back in camp I put Freddie to bed. He remained there for several days and his condition slowly began to improve.

chapter 11

THE LAND WAS flooded by the golden brilliance of the mid-afternoon sun. Heat waves rose in trembling layers. The usual murmur of the bush had given way to a symphony of peace. Even a nearby hornbill had ceased its noisy call. This was the beginning of the silent hour—a period that occurs each day in the wilds when Nature's pulse relaxes and time stands still.

I went into the bush with Gara-Yaka to see whether her hunting skill had improved. The cheetah is mainly a daytime hunter; darkness aids the stealthy leopard who hunts alone, though the clannish lion too likes to take advantage of the night's murk.

Three hundred yards from the camp Gara-Yaka suddenly squatted and stared fixedly ahead. Nothing moved that I could detect, but I waited and watched. My cheetah lay on her stomach for almost a full hour surveying her surroundings. Then I saw. The bush pulse began to beat. First one, then a second impala ewe materialized from thick cover. A moment later several more of the ghost herd drifted into the open to graze. And then Gara-Yaka, who had waited so patiently, stalked, belly-creeping forward.

Sharing a view

She was using every bit of available cover in her mastery of camouflage, and when cover was lacking, she dragged herself forward with her claws, in itself a difficult feat. Her stratagem was clear: if she could advance to within striking distance, she would make her rush. Her method was perfect.

The symphony of peace and silence came to a close with rival male grasshoppers—like troubadours on trees—striking up their song, serenading their females to guide them toward themselves. I saw the females; they were listening. Picking their males by the resonance of the voice, they started to creep toward their chosen ones.

The breath of wind changed suddenly, as it often does in the bush; it ebbs and flows now in this direction, now in that. With its change, Gara-Yaka crept obliquely to the edge of a thicker line of bushes. Behind these she loped ahead a little way, still keeping well downwind. She was now about 50 yards from her quarry and almost ready to shoot forward in her swift death-rush.

But all her precautions to remain unseen were fruitless, for up went the head of a mature ram. Watchfulness means life in the wilds, both to the hunted and the hunters. Not for nothing did this ram have large horns like an Irish harp. Their sharp movement was a warning to the herd, which shot away in an instant, catapulted forward and upwind to a heavily wooded small valley, swerving in mild alarm and crashing through the bushes during their swift passage.

Gara-Yaka was off too. The valley was empty now except for the mature ram, who turned from his run and in three short leaps came back, face to face with the cheetah.

My cheetah was intelligent enough to know that her rush had been unsuccessful and she was ready to give up the chase. But she had not reckoned on the ram taking this stand against her. It must have been an entirely new experience for her. The ram reminded me of a bull in an arena, its legs planted stiffly, head down, sharp horns ready to gore the matador.

But the cheetah was not going to be gored! Though the ram swept his great horns in an arc and attacked with great speed, Gara-Yaka hurled herself sideways with the litheness of a matador. But she did get a fright, and though she emitted a snarl meant to be threatening, it was no more than a scared little boy's whistle in the dark. She turned and made a hasty retreat, coming back on the game trail, chastised and dejected, filled with the shame of failure.

When I stepped out and made my presence known to her, she bared her teeth at me and hissed. I spoke her

Start of a hunt

name softly. Then she knew me and reverted to her old affectionate self, rubbing her little face against my ankles.

Hardly had we walked a third of the distance back when a small herd of impala, probably a small section of the larger herd, crossed our path at about 80 yards. Most antelope stop to stare at whatever takes their attention before they dart off. I had timed them often and found the pause to be about three seconds. The small herd stopped and paused.

One, two, three, and the group was off again, leaping so beautifully that my cheetah was excited beyond endurance. From her walking pace she rocketed into a sprint. The impala were making for a sparsely wooded patch, just the kind of hunting place in which cheetahs revel. It all happened to order.

Gara-Yaka quickly chose her quarry. She flashed after it and brought it down in a cloud of dust. I paced out the distance she had gone to make her kill; her victim, a young ram, had had an 80 yards' start on her, and yet she brought him down in 150 yards!

First kill

When I arrived at the spot, I saw she was "loving" her kill. I had often noticed lionesses doing this. They lie close to the kill, resting their head on the victim. They purr, caress, and lick the carcass, with their ears flattened back, eyes half-closed, and a silly dreamy look on their faces. It may be some form of "showing-off" among carnivora, and perhaps also a form of "Be my guest" invitation to their families. On the other hand, it may be a cover-up for a highly excited state; and heaven help those who butt in to try to partake of the feast uninvited.

That night Gara-Yaka must have had a nightmare. I heard strange sounds coming from her basket. With my flashlight I saw her feet jerking in an action of pursuit. Little "wuffs" of excitement came from her throat, and her mouth moved, sucking and chewing. She was apparently reliving the hunt.

At first light she was out through the open window, and she was gone for the better part of the day. Toward sunset she came back to camp carrying a francolin in her mouth. The bird's feathers were wet with saliva and badly disheveled; either she had chewed it or had carried it a long distance by mouth. Gara-Yaka placed the bird at my feet and lay down, showing signs of exhaustion and grunting in a thin voice.

I felt her pads: they were throbbing and warm, probably having been much used during the eventful day. By all signs she must have had a field day. She followed with interest my examination of her, lifting her paws for me to get a better look, and licking the back of my hand. But she made short work of her toilet and was fast asleep without her usual evening fussing over me.

Very early the following morning she was gone again. I felt a pang of displeasure at her neglect of me. But as several chores had cropped up in camp, I turned my attention to these, leaving Gara-Yaka to her own amusement. A few elephant had been through the camp during the night, so silently that none of us had been aware of their presence. They had pulled the tops off my paw-paw trees and one of them had climbed into the low cement reservoir under the wind pump. His ample weight had cracked the cement base. The cement dam had to be repaired and I intended placing thorn fences around the paw-paw trees.

Freddie and Piet were there to assist me. Freddie still wore a bandage on his bitten finger and I noticed that the dressing was very soiled. It seemed to me he winced each time the finger touched an object, which I thought strange since he had not complained lately. And so I asked him to unwrap the bandage.

The end of the finger, with the fang marks still clearly visible, was a horrible sight. It was raw and greenish, and probably gangrenous. The nearest hospital was at Headquarters 140 miles away, but I decided to go immediately.

At the hospital my fears were confirmed. Freddie had gangrene, and his finger had to be amputated without delay. He remained in the hospital for several weeks because of the venom residue still in his system.

While I was at Headquarters I made my report about poachers to the District Commissioner and learned that poaching had reached proportions which threatened the very survival of several species of buck. The poachers were highly organized and slaughtered game on a very large scale; they were apparently supplying a thriving market adjoining the territory.

I was told of a recent incident in the western desert land where white poachers had penetrated more than 100 miles into the territory and afterward made a dramatic escape with three game-laden trucks. A fourth truck broke down and was abandoned by the poachers in the heat of the police chase. This vehicle contained more than 500 pounds of eland flesh and several sackfuls of dry biltong.

Poachers ridicule the regulations aimed at the preservation of game. They play a constant mocking hide-and-seek with the police. But the size of their areas of operation makes it very difficult to control these bands of thieving butchers.

chapter 12

ON THE DRIVE back to camp without Freddie, I was heavily preoccupied. I had only been on the road some while when, on rounding a bend, I saw a car drawn up to the side of the road. A few seconds earlier I had heard hooting, and so I now slowed down to see if the occupants needed help. They were unaware of my arrival, all crowded to one side of their vehicle. It was apparent that they were trying to attract the attention of someone or something in the bush, and seemingly they were successful.

There was a small herd of elephant about 50 paces off the road to the left—six bulls, an old cow with a half-grown calf, and another cow holding on to a tree, giving birth to a calf. One of the larger bulls responded to the hooting and detached himself from the circle of uncles and brothers guarding the mother-to-be.

The elephant raised his trunk like a periscope to scent the air. His huge, sail-size ears went stiffly out sideways. With a springy step he ambled forward toward the offending car. The occupants spilled out of the vehicle like apples from a basket and ran to a nearby koppie on the op-

The clan guarding the mother-to-be

posite side of the road. One of the men carried a rifle. I saw them clamber up the steep rocky rise and watch fearfully from there.

The bull looked up at them and trumpeted a couple of shrieking blasts. He raised his head high in suspicious inquiry and approached the abandoned car. His great trunk felt and sniffed the various parts while his feet stamped angrily. He completely ignored my Land Rover, and I sat quite still. This bull was a good 12 feet high.

He continued his examination of the car until he found fresh human scent. Then he went berserk! He trumpeted shrilly and charged the car piercing the radiator with his tusks. Extricating them, he lifted the car high and smashed it down, causing it to bounce like a great ball. The now dislodged hood was ripped completely off and hurled away like a piece of cardboard. Such beastly fury I had never before witnessed. He was, by now, intent on utter destruction of the metal monster that had annoyed him so. Again and again he lifted the car like Gara-Yaka would the ball. Finally he butted the side with his monstrous head, thereby reducing the vehicle to a mangled mess.

At this stage the man with the rifle apparently recovered from his initial scare. He climbed down from his rock refuge and came a few paces forward, raising his rifle to his shoulder. The weapon seemed to be no more than an 8-caliber Mannlicher, far too light to be used against such a huge beast at a difficult three-quarter angle. The man was trying for a brain shot through the earhole.

The shot shook the elephant, but that was all. The animal only became more infuriated. Leaving the wrecked car, the bull turned on the man. It is a never-ending wonder to me how fast a seven-ton brute can run. In one second, while the man stood rooted in amazement, the big animal was practically on him. I knew the man would be doomed if I did not try to help. I ripped the .375 from its bracket and leaped out of the Land Rover. By now the bull had wrenched the rifle from the man and was trampling it to a twisted scrap.

I yelled loudly and the bull stopped. It turned and looked at me with what seemed mad eyes. Though elephants have poor sight, at such close quarters the monster must have seen me quite clearly. He hesitated momentarily and I aimed at the triangle formed by his bloodshot eyes and the beginning of his trunk. I squeezed the trigger as I prayed.

The huge head rocked as though struck by the fist of a giant and dust flew from the countless wrinkles on his skin; his front legs buckled and he went down on his knees; shuddering once, he rolled over on his side.

It was a good brain shot, but I was by no means proud of it. A magnificent wild colossus had to die because these careless people had not observed the warnings of experienced wild-life protectors. Needless to say, their car was a complete write-off.

During all this time the rest of the herd had not moved. The baby arrived and both mother and child were well. Slowly they started drifting away deeper into the bush, the little fellow following close behind his mother. It was slate gray and some baby! I looked at the disappearing giants and thought, "What will be their fate?"

The man's mouthing of thanks brought me back to reality. The sight of the cringing human being made me heartily sick. I offered to take the group back to town, but all the way I refused to utter a single word of conversation. I hoped to give them enough time to meditate on their folly and to realize why dangerous game should not be molested when it is behaving peacefully.

It is well known in the bush that peaceful and harmless game may become dangerous in given circumstances. Piet and I had gone to inspect one of the water holes, because most of our game lingered near these and the rivers at dry mid-winter. We watched the animals wading into the water to drink and to enjoy the coolness of the liquid around their hoofs. As these drinking places were used by all types of animals, they resembled bathing beaches.

Let no one think that it is only the domestic cats who preen and cleanse their coats. There is hardly a wild animal that is not more fastidious in the care of its body than an average human being. Even the frosty-faced vultures had their own private bathing spots, since they are friendless and despised by most of the other inhabitants of the wild. Much to my surprise they performed their ablutions daily, thus belying their epithet, dustbins of the bush!

The vultures came sailing out of the blue singly and in pairs, solemnly settling down by the water in the heat of the late morning. It looked as though dental hygiene was an important factor in vulture society, for their first act was to wipe and cleanse their beaks in the sand. I fancied hearing them gargle and mumble: "Oh, for a good mouthwash after that last stinking carcass!"

Then, standing like important company presidents faced with a vital issue, they contemplated the water with a scowl. At long length they strutted down to the water's edge in the manner of many a beach hero and took the plunge. Feathers ruffled, wings limp, they shook their bodies vigorously in the sandy water, rubbing their bald pates and necks on their shoulder plumage until they were clean according to vulture standards.

Once out of the bath, they again shook themselves, as dogs do on leaving water. Purified and wholesome again, the vultures flipped up to the bare branches of nearby

Vultures like baubles on a nude tree

trees and stood with wings wide open to dry. Much preening followed and every feather was fastidiously replaced to its rightful position.

Seeing all this I decided that vultures were, after all, quite nice members of bush society. Later, when I watched them soaring up into the sky with majestic sweeps, I looked upon them with a high regard which I had never felt before. Unhappily, this feeling lasted for only about ten minutes—until we came upon a score or more vultures voraciously gulping chunks of putrid flesh from a bushbuck they had found.

The ructions of a clash between rival tribes was nothing compared with the hopping and plunging of this madly fighting gang. They shoved forward with wings flapping, bouncing each other in their eagerness to be within picking reach of the delicacy. They struck away at those in a better position, beating up dust and filling the air with their squabbling squawks. In half an hour only the head and bones remained of the buck. Some of the muck-smeared individuals now began to depart in search of a further feast, or perhaps to rid themselves of the sickening odor in the cool water of their bathing pool.

But the few that remained seemed to be very occupied with something near a thorn bush. With the din of their violent outbursts lessened, we heard faint groans. Piet wrinkled his face inquiringly and turned his head to focus a small ear in the direction of the sound. He went into his typical fat-tailed Bushman crouch like a hound on the scent, slowly turning his face from left to right. Then he reached the thorn bush and pointed characteristically with his thumb at drag marks on the hard-baked earth.

My first impression was that the drag marks had been made by carnivores, but when I again heard the faint

Few hunters appreciate how dangerous the handsome bush-buck can become

groans I recognized them to be human. What was the owner of the voice doing in that thorn scrub?

We scared away the remaining vultures and prized up the fringe of the bush, bending away and cutting branches filled with three- to four-inch-long spikes. A coal-black native lay there helpless and bloodstained from obvious injuries. He repeated his moans again weakly. A small-bore rifle lay beside him. Piet sized up the situation with expert eyes and picked up two used .22 cartridge cases.

There, in the badly injured bloody mess and in the cartridge cases, was written the answer to my question: a harmless bush-buck; an inadequate weapon; a dangerous attack in retaliation; a tragedy!

Driving hastily back to camp with the victim, I was occupied by the thought that so few hunters appreciate how extremely dangerous this handsome Bambi-type of animal can become when wounded or cornered. Although it is one of the smaller species of antelope, a bush-buck ram can grow to quite a good size. When this basically shy buck has been aroused by provocation, it shows its fierce courage, for it is an animal not only outstanding in appearance but remarkable in character. It has often been known to attack its tormentor, human or predator, and has frequently been the humiliation and even death of many of its hunters. Seemingly this was a good example.

The half-dead man had been bleeding profusely from deep wounds inflicted by the sharp, twisted, dagger-like horns of the buck. We cut away much of the blood-soaked clothing that had dried hard on his injuries. To my great surprise, he turned out to be "one of our old clients." Piet at once recognized him as one of the party of snare-laying poachers we had caught red-handed some months back. It seems he did not want to reform; once a poacher always a poacher!

Now he lay limp on the camp bed, breathing weakly and looking ashen despite his coal-black complexion. Since he could not have survived the 140-mile journey to the hospital, I consigned his soul to the waiting spirits of his ancestors.

But some of the natives of southern Africa are made of tough fiber. A shot of brandy between his locked jaws brought him back from the grave. Indeed, he almost rose up from the bed to follow the cup for more of the potent elixir. A second swig was as good as a shot in the arm, and it put him on the road to recovery.

Some hours later he felt strong enough to tell us about his life-and-death struggle with the bush-buck. He described how he fought the enraged animal with his bare hands, as it plunged its horns repeatedly into his body.

And along with this story, he told us of his career—one not
unusual among these people who live on the fringes of the
Bushland.

He was called Wilson, named by his father after a
famous person beyond the waters of the sea. He was a
Muvenda originating from the Zoutpansberg in the northern Transvaal. From his story it was clear that his was a
restless character, for he had wandered far and wide to
the Kalahari in the west and Tongaland on the east coast.
He made no secret of the fact that he was just a bit more
than fond of liquid refreshment and strong tobacco.

During his sojourn in Mozambique he came across some
Indians who engaged him as a servant boy. They practiced
oriental magic, especially snake-charming, and this greatly
attracted Wilson's attention. He often spied on their activities to learn their secrets, until one day he was caught
and received a thrashing within an inch of his life. For
this he stabbed the head of the family to death and made a
quick getaway.

From the pocket of his ragged clothing he pulled out
a small beaded bottle which contained some old snake
fangs and a powder made from the roots of trees. He in-
formed us it was good "muti"—medicine—for poisonous
snake bites. With the demonstrative flair of a magician he
showed us how the "muti" worked. First he scratched his
arm with a snake fang and then rubbed in the powder.
Yes! He lived!

My first reaction was to regret that he had not been at
hand with his "muti" when Freddie was bitten.

But then I realized that the fang had obviously knocked
about with him for some time, and so even if it still contained some venom, it would long since have lost its
potency. Here was an impressive demonstration that was

just good hoodwink, as Wilson's own experience had proved—according to the rest of his story.

He had bought himself a wife and had settled down. Some devil in him made him fancy that he could become a "nganga"—witch doctor—and cash in by the snake-muti game. He collected poisonous snakes and drew their fangs for stock-in-trade. He had forgotten, however, one basic fact—that certain snakes regrow their lost fangs!

Somehow one of his captives escaped one night and brought tragedy into his business. The snake bit his wife and small son, both of whom died in spite of the administration of the magic white powder! This terrible loss set Wilson footloose again, to seek and find solace in hard liquor, which in the course of his varied assignments as house-boy, farmhand, cobbler, smith, and mechanic came his way.

From his assorted masters, he had picked up a good knowledge and had become quite skilled in these trades, and eventually he even understudied a genuine witch doctor. But the restless hand of fate threw him in with some idlers, who gladly utilized his many abilities and adapted these for game poaching. And so it was that the law caught up with Wilson in the shape of Freddie and Piet. For six months he had cooled his heels in jail.

When I questioned him about his latest unlawful visit to the game reserve he unashamedly admitted that he had come to take revenge on Freddie and Piet. He said he had enough money on his release from jail to buy a stolen .22 rifle with a handful of cartridges. He was on his way to our camp when he saw a large bush-buck ram hardly more than 30 paces away.

This was real temptation—far stronger than any poacher worthy of the name could resist—and so he raised his rifle

and shot. While he told me this he became so excited that
he switched from one language to another; we had difficulty in following him. In my honor he spoke mainly in
English, but when at a loss for a word he helped himself
in Afrikaans, Chivenda, Sechwana, Zulu, and Shangaan,
together with dialects we merely guessed at. He boasted
of speaking 14 languages, but not one correctly, I gathered.

Wilson invariably prefaced his sentences with the word
"wenchus," which I took to be some obscure dialect, but
which turned out to be simply "King's English," meaning
"when just . . ."

So "wenchus" he fired at the buck, the buck charged at
him. As it came on him, he jumped aside and fired again,
scoring another hit. The buck bounced past, turned
around, and, with its white dorsal crest erect like a Mo-
hican's hair, it charged again.

The bush-buck banged into Wilson's defensively out-
held rifle and knocked it out of his hands, at the same time
hooking one of its horns into the man's thigh. Wilson
grabbed the buck's horns with both hands and that was
when the life-and-death struggle began in earnest. Man
and animal rolled over on the ground like a pair of wres-
tlers, while Wilson was repeatedly gored deep in the
stomach and in the chest.

The native was too scared to let go of the horns for
fear that the buck "wenchus free" would tear him wide
open. He held on with every ounce of energy he could
muster and slowly climbed onto the back of the fighting
animal and lay across it. To his relief, after a while, he
could feel the buck growing weaker and quieter, and so
released his hold and retrieved his rifle.

He shot the almost victorious opponent through the
head, but he could not attend to himself, for he was so
weak from loss of blood that all he could do was to crawl

under the thick thorn canopy for shelter against vultures and carnivores.

He now lay back, with something like a penitent expression on his face. He closed his eyes and no amount of swishing the brandy bottle under his nose would bring him round again. He remained recumbent for several days during which we treated his multiple wounds. Piet, however, assured me that Wilson would live.

True to this diagnosis, Wilson reported himself off the sick list in due course. Although immensely grateful for our attention and care of him, from there onward he took his treatment into his own hands. Dipping a vulture feather into hyena fat he scratched his wounds until eventually the healed scabs fell off.

All this time he looked so crestfallen, thin, and haggard that I forgave the fact that he had come on a mission of vengeance and had thrown in some poaching for good measure. I decided to try him out and offered him a cup of brandy, but I might as well have offered him some vile concoction, for he waved it politely but firmly aside. He seemed to be a completely changed man and made himself very useful in the camp. In the absence of Freddie I put him into uniform and employed him as Game Scout No. 3.

Only Gara-Yaka remained aloof toward Wilson, following his every step with a scowl. It was as though she could not forgive him for his part in the snare-laying which almost ended her life.

chapter 13

WILD ANIMALS are not always peaceable, and they are not always innocent victims of persecution. Among those who steal from man are the lion, leopard, baboon, hyena, and especially the elephant. Few of these will bypass the chance to take man's stock or his crops if they can. In my area three big landowners had at various times tried cattle ranching only to find their herds stampeded and halved in almost no time by lions. In one case, the cattle were scattered so far that the last one was recovered 52 miles away. I have come across many skeletons of cattle in the bush, the bones spread out in a circle of 30 to 40 feet in a grim mosaic.

Because elephants require an enormous quantity of food daily—about 400 pounds of greenery—they are notorious raiders of plantations and of native gardens. Many an elephant has turned rogue as a consequence of being wounded by a shot from a native defending his crops. The festering wound becomes the bane of the elephant's life, and the irritated animal will kill any humans—usually innocent ones—in his mad thirst for revenge.

Once I was detailed to be the judge and executioner

in a vendetta between a herd of elephant—one of which had turned nasty—and a small settlement of natives.

I was in thick bush above the Back-line, my northern boundary, with Gara-Yaka. A large colony of Crested Blue guinea-fowl lived in this part: excellent runners and dodgers when chased. I had to visit the area and had thought it would be good exercise for the plump Gara-Yaka to exert herself a little by flushing and catching some of these game-birds. And so we had wandered some distance into the thicket.

Gara-Yaka had caught four of these sly birds and we were returning to the path where I had left the car when I was startled by a loud and angry trumpeting. Only 20 yards away stood a giant of an elephant with only one tusk. He was an animal with a grudge and had set an ambush for me. He raised his trunk, trumpeted, and then charged toward me, a surly, ugly expression on his wrinkled leathery face.

As a rule the large hunting-cats and elephant leave each other severely alone: even the 600-pound lion will give a wide berth to the seven-ton "real" king of the jungle. But Gara-Yaka was unaware of this rule and had not yet profited by experience. Stupidly, she sat down on her haunches growling lion-fashion in a deep-chested, angry rumble which is generally accepted as an effective warning signal in bush language.

The ill-tempered giant pulled up and swerved in surprise, like an aged colonel affronted by an upstart private. Later, I could afford to laugh at the two animals' reactions, but just then the situation was anything but amusing. The elephant lowered its trunk and, as a hand feels in the dark, searched the ground for the cheetah's scent. Gara-Yaka snarled louder!

I carried only a 12-bore shotgun and was therefore

technically defenseless. Some professional hunters hold that a shot will turn away a charging elephant, but I was not willing to test this opinion. I jumped behind a tree for camouflage but realized at once that this was useless, for the beast was in my wind and kept on receiving my scent. An elephant's eyesight may be poor but his sense of smell is second to none. While this animal dithered because of Gara-Yaka's attitude, I swung around and ran. I could still hear the cheetah and the great one hurling threats at each other. I sped in a rough zigzag course through the Mopani bush in a desperate bid to put a goodly distance between the elephant and myself.

The light shotgun felt like a ton weight in my hand and its strap was catching here and there on "Wait-a-bit" thorn bushes, the spikes of which are quite as strong as barbed wire. Several times the gun was almost wrenched from my grip, while my clothes were ripped and my body gashed by the spikes.

My hopes for escape were returning when a hideous trumpet blast behind me told that the attacker was in hot pursuit. A hasty glance back confirmed my fears. Bushes were crashing flat and swaying as the beast advanced like a tornado. I raced on, wondering just how far I could run at this speed before the crazy devil caught up with me. Perspiration was trickling into my eyes and I felt that everything possible was hampering escape. My own snail's pace of ten miles per hour was no match against the elephant's 25 or 30, but the will to live was urging me on. Hazy thoughts of this being my last hunt passed through my mind.

Soon I was so exhausted that my legs refused to carry me farther, and my lungs were about ready to burst. Something inside of me said, "Turn the gun on yourself and deprive the monster of the pleasure of destroying you."

Then I found myself half falling, half running, legs dragging over the stones of a waterless tributary of the Shashi River. This part was familiar to me and I prayed that the stony bed of the river would slow down or stop my pursuer, for I knew that I was fast losing the race. Gara-Yaka had caught up with me, and I felt her brushing against my buckling legs.

It was good to know that my pal was there beside me whatever the result of the chase. I looked up to the river bank and saw cattle grazing there. In a last desperate effort I scrambled up the not too steep bank, thinking I would put the elephant off my scent if I could get beyond the cattle and my pursuer. Gara-Yaka now and then crisscrossed the elephant's path to divert it, but still it came thundering on.

I heard the terrified cattle scattering behind me, and I thought I should fall flat and hope that the giant would pass me by. Just then there appeared, like an oasis in the desert, a group of native huts about a hundred yards ahead. Would I make the settlement or would I be killed on their doorstep? With one last spurt of energy, I rushed and dived into the nearest hut, landing exhausted on the floor with pains in my labored lungs.

I lay there too numb to care whether I would be trampled to death. I just wished the ordeal over. Through my dazed mind there came a shrill, blood-curdling scream; vaguely I wondered if it were mine. There was some more frightful trumpeting and steam-engine blowing. By now I was hardly conscious. Could I be dead? Then waves of sanity returned and I realized I was breathing the stale air of the grass hut. I tuned my ears to catch sounds, any sounds, so long as I could be sure that I was indeed in command of my senses. I heard dull thudding, like something being repeatedly struck against the ground.

With tremendous effort I dragged myself to the doorway, a typically tiny one, hardly big enough to admit a person, and I peered out. A sight so horrible met my eyes that I had to turn away. Through a red haze I saw the elephant with its trunk twisted around the neck of a native woman: he was smashing her to a pulp on the hard ground. He lifted the limp body, waved it like a flag, and crashed it down. A man dived into the hut, sending me rolling across the floor. He grabbed hold of an old muzzle-loader and fired from the small entrance at the maddened brute. The elephant dropped the mangled body and ambled, limping, into the surrounding bush followed by Gara-Yaka, who urged him on his way.

After all the agitation had subsided, the owner of the muzzle-loader told me that this particular single-tusker was the leader of a herd that systematically destroyed the kraal's vegetable gardens and also siphoned away most of the water supply. An elephant drinks on an average 40 gallons a day; with 20 animals in the herd the supply was now almost nonexistent. I found out from the man that he was the Headman of the kraal, and he begged me to help eradicate the menace.

My .375 Magnum was in the Land Rover, and so I decided after a rest to fetch it and to return to the kraal. The Headman assured me that the elephants would return at nightfall to continue their draining of the water supply and the destruction of the gardens. Gara-Yaka and I set out to find my vehicle. Twice I caught sight of the drifting elephant herd as we made our way through the bush. The cheetah's tail shot out straight like a ramrod when she scented them, but I was by no means fit or keen enough for another chase. We cautiously weaved our way through with as little noise as possible.

Eventually we reached the Land Rover and I sighed

They syphoned away most of the water

The supply was now almost non-existent

with relief as I slammed shut the door. I checked the rifle
and loaded it with solid-nose bullets. We were loudly
welcomed by the villagers when we arrived back at the
kraal.

With as little delay as possible I outlined my carefully
thought-out plan to the Headman and his people. We all
set out to work preparing an effective welcome for the
killers should they threaten the village. The whole population was sent out to gather tinder-dry brushwood. We
had the wood placed in a circle around the village, with
spokes, as in a wheel, leading from between huts to the
center where a communal fire burned. Beside this fire, I
parked the car.

The circle was left open where the path entered the
kraal. This was the only entrance, and we hoped the elephants would use it to walk into the trap. The dry grass
and brushwood spokes centered near the fire could be
easily ignited by one person. The burning circle would
protect the kraal and provide illumination for counter-
action.

Thus set, the villagers were ordered to their huts and
commanded to silence. There was actually little need for
these orders. They were all dumb with anticipated terror.
Only the Headman and I, with Gara-Yaka, remained in
the center. My cheetah gave repeated evidence of her dislike for the nearness of the native, and so I moved him
downwind from her to stop her fussing. Crickets chirped
their monotonous song.

Venus and the Orion constellation must have wheeled
about halfway on their routes when the cheetah raised
her head and began staring intently at the dark bush. I
thought I heard a rustle, and then a twig snapped. She
growled, and I rubbed the short hairs under her chin to
console her. She started to purr loudly, a comforting

sound in this eerie setting. The memory of my ordeal of only a few short hours earlier was still very vivid in my mind, and I must admit that I was scared.

In one of the shallow wells to my right, a frog croaked a sinister warning which ended abruptly. Something was passing the well. The continuously chirping crickets also fell silent—as if they knew something was about to happen. Gara-Yaka grew tense and ceased her purring. The Headman rolled his eyes half in signal, half in fear. I fervently hoped that I still appeared dignified and confident though I felt far from being either! Quietly I slipped off the safety catch of the rifle; this gave me a feeling of protection.

I thought of the giants now encircling us—a herd of normally well-behaved animals which had now turned vicious. I also thought of the drollness of the situation in which I found myself: here was I sitting—waiting—to protect people from animals, when my calling was exactly the reverse.

Gara-Yaka stood up, her forelegs stiffly planted and her hind legs half-crouching. Her face and ears wedged forward. She ducked her head and lifted it again, peering as though to penetrate the surrounding darkness. Then she slunk back about three steps in a frightened way, making a few switches with her tail. The elephants were near! It was time to put our defenses into operation. I firmly believed the elephants would not attack through a circle of leaping flames. I nodded to the Headman.

Like a ghost, the man placed a blazing brand to each of the brushwood spokes. The dry twigs and grass caught like gunpowder. In seconds yellow fingers of flame ran along the circle of the perimeter like a Saint Catherine wheel on Fireworks Day.

A moonless bush is as dark as a bottomless pit. Now the

quickly spreading light cast by the fire enabled us to see
beyond the boundary of the kraal. At a swift glance I saw
nine or ten elephants frozen into statues by the sudden
fire. They were in various stages of advancement into the
kraal—some with trunks up, scenting, all with ears standing stiffly out to catch every sound of counterattack or of
flight. They were motionless and very silent. A pretty picture—under different circumstances.

The herd was waiting for their leader's decision. I
looked around for Gara-Yaka. She had taken refuge between the rear wheels of the car, ready to make a break
for it. In her fright she now uttered one of those bird-like
chirping sounds which always so amused me. A twitter-
chirp from a large cheetah sounds quite ridiculous.

We had previously arranged that at a signal from the
Headman all adults would rush out of their huts, grab a
burning brand, and hurl it at the nearest elephant if the
herd attempted to rush the kraal at the sight of humans.
Apparently the villagers took Gara-Yaka's chirp for the
signal, and they poured out making such pandemonium
that it would have done justice to a community twice
their number.

The sight of yelling humans so incensed the herd that
they charged immediately, and the natives did as instructed and cast the burning torches at the advancing
elephants. The crucial moment had come, and now was
the time to strike fear into the herd and to teach them a
lesson. I caught glimpses of large gray-black bodies turning and running with that curious swing of their thick
girths. Some stood petrified at the sight of the fire; others
stamped the ground and whipped about with their trunks.
They seemed more hesitant and much less aggressive than
before, which was to the credit of our plan.

I tried to guess what the effect would be if I fired a

THE STORY OF A CHEETAH 119

shot at them. Something held me back. Behind me, human screaming increased in volume, and when I turned to look for the cause I found it was no victory yell. There was a dark unlit gap where the fire had already died down and through this gap a large elephant came charging into the kraal. It had only one tusk! My enemy, the leader. The hysterical, bewildered natives milled in all directions. Some took refuge behind me, using me as a shield, while others clustered close to the car and some flattened themselves under it; these were snapped at and cuffed by Gara-Yaka, but they preferred Gara-Yaka to being trampled to death by the looming monster. It seemed all hell had broken loose. I felt a horrible sensation of fear lest I should fail in my task. My heart beat so loudly that I could feel its throb in my left foot.

I took as good aim as the flickering light would permit, sighting low, for darkness tends to make one overshoot, and I fired. There is something reassuring about the metallic click of the empty cartridge case clattering on the ground, and of a fresh shell sliding into the breach. But there was no need for a second shot. The bull crumpled, his outstretched trunk almost touching my shoe. I had settled my score with him.

The remainder of the herd slipped away, thoroughly beaten. These intelligent animals know man and rifle, and they recognize death too. Soon they all disappeared into the night—for good—never again to molest this unfortunate kraal, as was just.

Fear and misery now turned to joy and jubilation. The drums started beating and the people danced a barbaric routine around the communal fire. The older women prepared a feast, for there were tons of meat. In the morning I had the tusk cut out. It weighed nearly 65 pounds, and I handed it to the District Commissioner with my report.

chapter 14

I HAVE RELATED the previous events to show, as I said, that animals are not always blameless in their actions. Strangely, they seem to know they are doing wrong when they raid farms. I have heard that lions especially have a guilty conscience after raiding cattle paddocks or thorn enclosures for goats.

There was, for instance, the case of the young lion, a member of the same pride in which Gara-Yaka's pet aversions, Sheila and Moll, the two lionesses, were the "young ladies" of the family. This young male, mature and powerful, the son of the patriarch of the pride, was permitted to hang around so long as he did not show undue interest in the females.

But Nature has its ways. The Old Boy must have caught the young one in warm courting, for a frightful battle ensued in which age, skill, and ferocity were pitched against youth, brute strength, and enthusiasm. The old gentleman eventually gained the upper hand and would have killed his son had not the youngster taken refuge in flight.

The refugee came and loitered around our camp, bad-

tempered, making a nuisance of himself by creeping up on
Gara-Yaka and rousing her from her slumber as he grunted
a challenge. Mutt and Jeff and the pups gave the alarm by
squawking and barking in turn when they spotted the
lion. The noise-despising young swain then angrily decamped.

His square-humped run proved his anger, and I sympa-
thized with him. Striped with smarting slashes, his fur
coated with dry blood, lonely and unfed, he was really
out to make trouble. He was, in addition, tormented by a
host of pestering flies, and all this was enough to raise
anybody's temper. Papa had certainly given him a good
corrective plastering. I called a very reluctant Gara-Yaka
to accompany me to trail the lion; only after much coaxing
and begging did she finally consent to come.

The lion was hot on the spoor of a troop of zebra and
wildebeest which had earlier been grazing in that direction. I could almost see his mouth slavering at the thought
of feasting on one of those striped horses of the bush. The
afternoon was perfectly still. Not a breath of breeze
stirred even a blade of grass—a bad situation for hunting.

We trailed the lion to a koppie where he suddenly
crouched low, having seen the zebra. They were grazing
beyond a line of bush bordering a wooded ravine. There
was a magnificent stallion lording it over a harem of mares
with foals of varied vintages. Unluckily for them, the
wildebeest had gone on much farther, for those grotesque
creatures are watchful and quicker to scent danger than
other animals.

A little whisper of wind came up as though to assist
the lion. It confirmed to him that his quarry was indeed
zebra, for in the bush scent is quite as important as sight,
if not more so. He stalked down the koppie side from cover
to cover, pausing behind a shrub, then lying along a patch

of tall grass for a few seconds, getting nearer and ever
nearer to his quarry.

Then he attacked. His charge was awkward. The young
fool had selected the great stallion when there were tender
mares and succulent foals for the having! Whether it was
his temper, his greed, or a subconscious effort to regain for
himself some of the self-respect he had lost is difficult to
say. The fact is, the proud stallion was far too experienced
for the young lion. With a loud snort, the zebra jumped
aside.

The lion landed insecurely on the stallion's shoulder,
his claws and arms not having the necessary grip to pull
the quarry down. I could see he would never make the kill,
for the zebra bucked and kicked like a rodeo bronc and
bounced like a yo-yo. The lion's claws were already slip-
ping when the stallion reared up and dislodged his unwelcome rider. The lion fell close to the zebra's back hoofs,
and I winced. The stallion smashed its two steel-tough
hoofs into the youngster's belly. I heard his tortured and
winded grunt as he rolled into the nearby bush out of the
path of the furious stallion.

Gara-Yaka watched the drama with as much interest as
I. She was ready to charge into the fray had I not restrained
her by putting my arms tightly around her neck. She all
but dragged me with her.

The lion got up, shook himself, and muttered with an
asthmatic catch in his throat, grumbling undoubtedly at
his bad luck, the difficulties of a lone hunt, probably even
over the hardness of life in general, for a solitary hunter
never fattens. He tossed up his head, his mane waving,
and gave vent to his feelings in a tremendous solo. The
deep roars were interspersed with grunts as he paused to
catch his breath, then rolled over the bushland, scaring

every buck for miles around. His humiliation and the pangs of hunger rankled in him.

He started off in a southerly direction, and while Gara-Yaka and I were returning to camp, I thought of the lone one and named him the Prodigal. Because of his love-quest the Old Boy had pushed him out of the pride, ending his days of easy kills and full feeds. Until he could form a pride of his own those happy days would remain just a memory, and it might take a long time; meanwhile, he must survive!

This is usually the time when "youths" of lionhood, each expelled from the family circle for some misdeed or other, band together for mutual protection and support. This is also the time when many of them perish through malnutrition and injuries received from faulty tackling of powerfully horned quarries, or, quite often, get killed by other lions onto whose territories they have strayed and been caught "poaching."

The Prodigal would be cautious now on his southbound drift, not looking for any new hazards after the sledge-hammer kick in his midriff. Although I strained my ears, I did not hear his voice during the night.

About noon the next day a cyclist brought a report of a lion raid on the cattle paddock near our southern boundary. He had noticed that the lion's fur was matted with blood when he and his dogs had tracked it down to where it lay sleeping under a tree. Nearby was the carcass of a young cow. About 20 pounds of flesh had already been stripped off, and he said that this lion was the shyest and most self-conscious one he had ever seen. It seemed to him that the lion was groaning as though suffering pain. I knew the raider to be our delinquent, the Prodigal. He had traveled 15 to 20 miles during the night and had made his kill of a defenseless cow.

Though I went after him, I secretly did not blame the youngster for this deed. I too had been chastised by my father in my youth, and I knew the shame of it. His first independent hunt had ended in a fiasco, and so injury had been added to injury. He had to eat and he had the right to live! Who would cast the first stone?

The messenger did. It was to flush the lion from a dense clump of bushes where the pups and Gara-Yaka had spoored him. A succession of coughing grunts rumbled from what seemed to be deep down his bulging stomach. They grew in crescendo to a wild riot of thunderous frightening sounds. He whirled out of cover, a wonderful example of "No holds barred." He probably thought the pups and Gara-Yaka were after his meat, but when he spotted the messenger and me, he froze in his tracks, skulked backward into the safety of the bush, then turned and dashed away. His shyness and guilt-awareness over the kill were clear to see.

By some quirk of fate the father of the Prodigal had led his pride on a thieving escapade in the south, raiding for goats, although there was an abundance of game in their own area farther north. The five of them killed 20 goats in an orgy that was not characteristic of lions hereabouts. The second night, as was expected, the pride returned to dine on the left-overs of the slain goats. Two white hunters lay in wait, and each shot one of the pride. The great black-maned father himself was one of the victims and the other an old lioness. We easily identified the Old Boy by the unhealed wounds he had received from his son when they had the big fight. His magnificent pelt is today adorning a wall of his vanquisher.

The young delinquent had now fled northeastward and had probably picked up the scent of his family who were beating a hasty retreat. He joined them and found he had no opposition. The events of the past few days, and the experience he had gained, had "made a man of him," and he was accepted as leader of the pride. He led them back northward, home, at a sloppy, high-humped shamble of two and a half miles per hour, his strong muscles standing out under his loose, slow-slipping hide.

The Prodigal knew well the dangers of the southern areas. There were cattle and goats for the taking, but death lurked behind this easy meat.

Now he had his own pride, and with them he could enjoy life to the full. A warm sunbath, a shady tree after a full feed—the lion's share and the King's privilege.

The wind changed, and the new squire turned his great head and looked for a while in our direction. He raised his beautiful scarred face, sniffed the air, and brought forth a deep grunt of what seemed to me utter satisfaction. Then he started off on his way, perhaps a little faster than before. But the two young lionesses, Sheila and Moll, turned back. They made a sudden and unexpected rush for Gara-Yaka, who was nearest to them. I fired a shot in warning, and though they ignored the shot, they wheeled around and loped off to join the pride when their new lord and master grunted a reprimand at them. For some time we could hear his swearing—he obviously knew better.

Fortunately, I had a chance to take a good look at the two young lionesses. It was clear that they were sisters, one a little larger than the other, both about two years old. I had learned to judge lions by their expressions, for they are very much like humans in that respect: one can see a nervous one, a surly one, many a good-natured one, and of course the nasty, mean types. These two girls were cheeky and provocative, much like their two-legged counterparts in the cities of man. It grieved me to think of them falling to guns as their father had.

chapter 15

THE DAYS GREW hot and silent, and the nights lost some of their biting cold. The vast expanse of bushland was dry and dusty with only a strip of green vegetation marking the edge of the open waterless river courses. Winter was on the way out and summer would soon follow. Then heavy rains would come and the bush would be a sight so beautiful to behold that it would be hard to remember the dusty dry bushes and faded grass.

Freddie returned to the camp none the worse for his unpleasant experience except, of course, minus a finger. His best friends became the Toppies, the conical-helmeted small dark birds that disclose the presence of snakes hidden in the bush or grass.

These lively birds are avowed enemies of snakes. The moment a reptile is spotted they gather in flocks of up to six and keep up an incessant din of chattering near the place where the snake lies. There were not many snakes around our parts, but we always took heed of the Toppies' warnings and went along to find and dispose of dangerous reptiles.

It was not always the poisonous snakes which were the

menace; poor Gara-Yaka nearly fell victim to a python one day. Through the bush telegraph I had received news of poaching activities in the eastern corner of the land, around the confluence of the Shashi with the Limpopo. Little-used paths enabled game thieves to cross over the dry sandbed of the Shashi and to make capital of the herds usually concentrated there.

Freddie, Piet, and Gara-Yaka accompanied me on patrol. We made camp on a typically sandy spot near the Shashi. Soon after our arrival, we discovered a colony of pythons. They are invariably housed in ant-bear holes, and their presence is betrayed by their regular furrow-like spoor, marking their passage to and from the holes. But we had come to trap poachers, and therefore paid only scant attention to the pythons.

This was a particularly wild and well-stocked game area. Among the visitors that strayed through our camp were young buck, tortoises, and porcupines, as well as a variety of unwelcome insects, especially ticks.

For several days we had crisscrossed the bush on foot, looking for the telltale circle of vultures that might betray poachers' activities. After a tedious period of lying watchfully in hot sand and perching on the tops of tall trees, I decided to take a dip in a rock pool that had received its water from a tiny spring. The large rock basin held comparatively clear, unmuddy water, unlike most water holes in the bush.

Gara-Yaka accompanied me, and—hating water—she remained seated on the bank above the pool, looking around with her usual alertness. I knew her "Ungh" would warn me of approaching prowlers. I had been in the water for only a few minutes when I happened to glance toward the cheetah to note her reaction to my immersion. But she was not there! The rock she had been sitting on lay bare and immobile as it probably had for hundreds of years—a silent witness to the mystery and lore of the bush.

There was no response to my repeated calls. As she was always very self-willed and independent in her actions, I thought she might have seen something of greater interest than a man bathing, and had probably wandered off to investigate. Nevertheless, I did not fancy a long bath without knowing her whereabouts. So I waded out of the pool and heard her high-pitched meaow followed by a faint, drawn-out gurgle. The sound came from close by.

I dashed up the bank expecting to see her with a young antelope she had caught while it was drinking from the pool. Instead, I found her on the ground with a good-sized python wrapped around her.

Gara-Yaka tried to free herself of the smooth writhing loops ringing her body. The reptile had my cheetah's face in its mouth, silencing her and suffocating her while its shiny muscular coils were working over her like turning wheels. It appeared that the snake was endeavoring to lever itself over with its tail, to roll down to the pool. Gara-Yaka's strong legs were helplessly held by the coils.

There were no suitable sticks at hand, and I could not use my rifle so I picked up a rounded stone which had been smoothed by centuries of rolling in water. With this I struck the snake once, twice. It released Gara-Yaka's head and hissed menacingly at me. The great coils writhed.

Securing a good grip on the reptile's neck I forced its beastly head down to a rock below and struck it again and again. Only after these blows did it relax its hold on Gara-Yaka. I did not want to kill it, so I gave it another blow as a warning and then backed away. Pythons have a set of strong recurved teeth with which they inflict nasty though nonvenomous bites. The reptile felt beaten and started to glide away. It had been sufficiently punished.

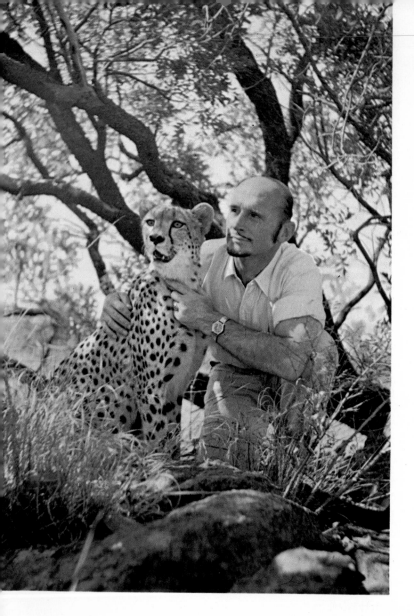

Gara-Yaka with the author

My cheetah soon regained most of her composure and showed only the discomfort of bruised ribs. I examined her and found no fractures. Had I failed to hear her cry or delayed the rescue, she would surely have been rolled into the water, drowned, and then crushed by the python.

The sandy banks of the pool, leading down to the Limpopo River, were covered here with coarse long grass in which a snake could easily lie in wait. The ever-watchful Gara-Yaka had probably seen the snake and, true to her customary curiosity, had gone to investigate. The python, it seemed, had permitted her to approach to within striking distance, and then had thrown itself at my pet, coiling her up with lightning speed and, using the favored method of pythons, seizing the victim by its mouth to smother it first. At times a python will hide itself in water with hardly more than a nose-tip showing above the surface until an unwary animal strays to within lunging distance.

This was the first time I had seen a python attack a carnivore; their usual diet consists mainly of the smaller mammals—dassie, hare, duiker, and baboon. Of course francolins and guinea-fowl are favorite delicacies. Undoubtedly, even bigger animals are within the python's power to capture and to disable. These larger game, however, must first be squeezed almost to a pulp before being swallowed head first. After such a feast the python becomes very lethargic for days and even weeks during the digestive process. But this attacker was ready to eat again.

I considered myself extremely fortunate that the victim on this occasion was not I, for Gara-Yaka could not have helped me. I knew of a few cases in which men had come off second best in their encounter with pythons, but this was my first close brush with Africa's largest snake.

I took the cheetah back to camp, and on the way I

noticed the blood oozing from the punctures left by the reptile's fangs on her face. These I treated, Gara-Yaka purring loudly her approval.

Tracking down the poachers proved a more complicated business than at first anticipated. We noticed several schools of vultures circling over different areas, but when we reached these places, we found only the signs of the activities with the culprits gone. They moved about quickly, slaughtered the game, and then withdrew to a new area. It was galling, for obviously they were aware of our presence. The vastness of the area was distinctly in their favor.

For a day or two after the attack on Gara-Yaka, she was her old affectionate self, rubbing faces with me, brushing my legs, leaning on me and asking for caresses. The moment I sat down she would place her paws on my shoulders and touch her nose to mine in an "Eskimo kiss" followed by rough licking of my forehead.

One hears much of the fetid breath of carnivorous animals. Gara-Yaka was not guilty of this offense. Her breath was always clean and sweet. This may have been because of her diet of fresh meat and her weekly ration of cod-liver oil. I never hesitated to exchange nose-rubbing kisses with her, for she took these for granted. I had now graduated from foster father to something like a buddy, a commissar of fun, and a provider of food and frolic all in one.

On the second evening after the python attack on her, she was exceptionally charming in her manner. She had gone through the whole gamut of her repertoire of endearments, so much so that I sat up to take notice. I had been rubbed against, kissed, licked, and smeared with saliva. She always had a slight drool on her lips which gave them a shiny black appearance. I reciprocated these expressions of love with a tight hug and a firm chucking under the chin. Now, while hugging her, I noticed a faint odor of which I had not previously been aware.

Reflecting on this, it occurred to me that she appeared far more restless than before. Like a courting cat she brushed against bushes, lifted herself up off her forelegs like a dolphin emerging from the sea, then went down again only to reappear a little distance ahead. She was ill-tempered at times too now, cuffing and gently biting when the mood took her.

A few days later she walked along one of the game-paths intersecting the camp, and stood there contemplating and looking at me. Her tail swung from side to side strik-ing her flanks as though inducing her to make a serious decision. Her purr was as loud as that of a motor-scooter engine.

She picked her way along the path, then stopped, turned and looked at me, came back, only to walk away again. I knew she was inviting me to go for a walk. These walks had become routine since her cubhood. We usually made them in the late hours of the afternoon—during the cheetah hunting period. It was at this time, near nightfall in python-littered, leopard-haunted areas we knew little of, that I was not at all keen for a walk. One can stroll out of camp nine times out of ten and return unharmed, but there is always the tenth chance that something will hap-pen, and in the bush things happen suddenly and very unexpectedly.

Gara-Yaka was now two years old and in the full bloom of pretty feminine cheetahood. Her eyelashes were long and upcurved and they gave a depth of expression to her large jasper eyes. She had strange eyes: they looked at me coldly and superciliously at times, like those of a well-fed

Portrait of a Star

cat, and, at other times, with the mistrustful stare of a
wildcat. Yet, very often, she gazed at me with the faithful,
adoring eyes of a self-enslaved dog for his master.

This day she peered at me provocatively. To show that
my acceptance or refusal of her invitation did not matter,
she raised her tail in a most unfeminine way—like a tomcat—and squirted a jet at the nearest tree trunk. This surprised me, for she always made water in a very female-cat
manner, by squatting.

By all these unusual demonstrations, it had now become
quite clear to me that she was in season. I decided to go a
little way to find out what she wanted to show me. Every
few yards she stopped to spray the bushes, uttering a little
miaow and leaving a slight acrid scent hovering on the
light evening breeze.

Then she gave her "Ungh" signal, the one that meant
she had seen or heard something. She lay down on the
path watching intently. I drew behind a tree and stood
perfectly still, looking along the line of her muzzle. I
could see nothing in the gathering gloom. She remained
in this attentive position, ears pricked forward, for some
time. This signified that she was watching something of
great importance.

I strained my eyes to discover what held her attention,
but still I could see nothing. Then, on the warm, still,
evening air came the call of a cheetah. The sound was
deeper, more mature, and altogether more defined a voice
than that of Gara-Yaka. The sound had given me the
caller's direction. When Gara-Yaka heard the call, she
tensed and her nostrils dilated passionately. The last few
black rings on her tail and the white tuft at the end jerked
about as though suddenly electrified.

Emerging from cover was a beautiful large male cheetah.
He advanced a few paces toward Gara-Yaka, and they

Emerging from cover was a beautiful large male cheetah

looked at each other with suspicion as wild game do. But I detected recognition and friendliness showing through this Romeo's look. Though his demeanor was stern, he appeared pleased at the sight of Gara-Yaka. Then he advanced still closer and I heard soft sounds of conversation between them.

There was no point in remaining behind the tree, for darkness was rapidly enveloping the bush and I had to find my way back to camp. As I came out from my hiding place, I heard Romeo's fast intake of breath and the loud exhalation which was usually the prelude to a rumbling growl. He was voicing his objections to my presence. I did not blame him: I was the intruder.

Gara-Yaka lay staring at Romeo, her tail outstretched to full length with only the tuft twitching. She appeared to be mesmerized and completely oblivious of my presence.

By all signs it was indeed time to go. Normally she would have followed or made short rushes forward to ambush me from bushes and trees. Now she remained, letting me go without giving me even a backward glance.

My pet spent the night out in the bush. Freddie and Piet merely smiled knowingly when I told them the cause of Gara-Yaka's absence. Their expressions told me they thought this to be the termination of my friendship with my cheetah. The call of nature had proved stronger than her affection for me.

For this eventuality I had long prepared myself. Despite our close bond, she was still a daughter of the wild who had only half forsaken the ways of her kind for the association of a friendly human. She was still very much a wild animal. I had always known that whatever domestic ways she had acquired would be left behind when the call of a mate reached her. It seemed the call had at last come.

Gara-Yaka and Romeo strolled into the bush on their honeymoon

chapter 16

SOON AFTER sunrise Piet pointed at the sky. There was a single black spot moving in tight circles, gradually coming lower and lower. It was a vulture that had spotted something which might provide breakfast, but could not yet partake of it because of activity around its prey. I had an idea that my poachers were up to something there, and so I decided to investigate.

With Freddie and Piet I drove out, heading in the direction of the vultures, the number of which had now increased to seven. We had to move fast to keep the direction before the winged scavengers settled down on trees, for in some parts of the wilds 100 yards' miss is as good as 100 miles. We crashed through the bush, laying it low.

Coming on a path wide enough to take the Land Rover, we soon found fresh tire tracks crossing the path and leading in the direction we were following. This coincidence struck me as rather strange then, but in the heat of being at last on a solid quest I paid little further attention to the thought. It appeared on face value that the cunning and circumspect poachers had now cast all caution to the winds. Probably feeling secure, they appeared to defy

136

the law in their greedy business of extermination. They would have killed Gara-Yaka for her pelt if they could have set their sights on her, and the very thought of this urged me on.

A mile or so farther, the winding path straightened out into a sandy stretch. This strip of about 200 yards long was bound on both sides by thick interwoven bush and trees. It was not unlike a long bowling alley, except that the ground was of deep, loose sand into which our tires sank; the vehicle sidled for lack of grip. But the poachers' tracks led us along this trail.

We all saw it at once—an impala strung by its hind legs on a tree and two men working on it, apparently skinning the carcass. They had their backs to us and, surprisingly, had not heard the whine of our engine—or so I thought. I accelerated, and we went plunging and sidling through the sand. I was exulted that we had at last caught up with some of the poachers.

We were more than halfway through when they turned and stared. They moved as though to make a quick getaway. Again I accelerated. Two sharp hisses—like giant pythons hissing into an amplifier—came from the front of the car and it sagged, completely anchored. The back wheels churned the sand and the engine whined, then went dead.

As the three of us spilled out of the car, the two men pretended to scramble for their belongings close by. I ordered them to stand still, telling them that they were under arrest. In answer they raised their rifles and fired at us. One of their bullets thudded into the Land Rover; the other must have hit Piet, for he cried out.

We ducked for cover in pained surprise, and I fired a shot at the men. We had certainly been aware that we would be unwelcome when we met up with them, but none of us was prepared for such a hot reception. An engine somewhere roared into life; the two men darted into the bush and were gone before we could take another look at them. That was that!

Some of the vultures had settled on a high tree. At the report of the shots, they rose as one and heavily took to their wings, milling around confusedly.

I got up and impulsively raced forward in the forlorn hope of laying my hands on one of these aggressive game-thieves. I had gone only a few paces when I stumbled and fell headlong into the sand. My foot had caught on some object which was embedded in the soft earth.

Now I was fuming! I picked myself up and kicked at the object. I found it to be an impala horn buried deep, so that only its point showed on the surface. Now I knew what had happened to my two front tires! There must have been quite a minefield of these sharp horns concealed along the track.

I had to admit that it was a devilishly cunning stratagem, which savored somewhat of premeditated ambush and possibly murder. The poachers had purposely lured us here. Either they got cold feet or their shots went wild in their excitement. The shot meant for me hit the radiator, but passed through the upper part without causing irreparable damage. The heavy tires, however, were badly spiked and torn by the horns.

There was no way out: one of us would have to go back to camp, a good 15 miles away, to fetch the second spare tire, for I carried only one in the car. I patched up Piet's grazed shoulder and sent him back along with Freddie, who said he knew of a short cut to the camp.

When they had gone, I took stock of the situation. The time was nearly 8 A.M. With my trackers needing three and a half hours to reach camp and as much again to return, I would not have the tire until about three or four in the afternoon. To use up time, I changed one of the punctured tires for the spare and tinkered with the radiator, plugging it. The engine started up without any difficulty.

Later, I took a look at the tracks left by the poachers and saw where they had hidden their vehicle and where they had made their preparations for the ambush. The bait was the old smelly carcass of a sick impala, which they had hung to deceive us. Vultures had now been at it, scattering the loosening bones. Two jackals also arrived and fought with the scavenger birds for morsels from the carcass.

In the bush there is always much entertainment for those who wish to see and hear. A mixed herd of zebra and impala drifted into a nearby clearing, lazily cropping the small amount of grazing still left. Crickets sang their ceaseless song of "chee-ee-ee-se, chee-ee-ee-se," while wood-pigeons "coo-cook-ooh-ed" and a disturbed clutch of francolin broke out in hysterical cries of "ginger-beer, ginger-beer!"

I wandered back to my disabled vehicle, filling my lungs with the rich perfumed air of dry vegetation, watching thumbnail-sized blue, red, and green birds perform acrobatics, listening to the cheeky calls of the Koto-koto and Mukuwe birds. Through all these sounds, I detected the chatter of Toppies. The sound of their voices brought back thoughts of my cheetah. All at once I missed her terribly.

I wondered if she had been accepted by the stern-faced Romeo. I hoped heavy human scent on her had not lessened her chances for conjugal bliss. I worried that her non-return might have been caused by an attack or accident which had befallen her.

But I remembered how strong primary instincts were

Romeo, Prince of the Bushland

in the bush, and I felt it certain that the hard-faced lover
had espoused Gara-Yaka. Then, too, although she was
not fully matured, with her seven-foot length and 120-
pound weight she could well take care of herself. I had
long found that partly tame creatures like Gara-Yaka
could fully cope with the requirements of the wild bush—
by natural instinct.

Besides, for the moment my duties as guardian of my
cheetah had to be shelved for the more important ones of
arresting the poachers. So far every round had been won
by them. They must have thought me pretty dumb. As
chance often has more to do with such matters than the
best-laid stratagem, when ill-luck dogs one's trail it is best
to seek comfort in inactivity and relax.

I decided to prepare some food and then rest. It was an appealing idea to my famished stomach and my sore muscles. Since we were allowed by law ten antelope a month for the pot—a quantity we never used—I picked out an impala in the lingering mixed herd. The moment before I fired, a zebra passed with its head low and quite close behind my target. The shot was one of those flukes that may happen to a greenhorn, but is seldom achieved by the most experienced hunter. Now I had an impala and a zebra with one shot at 100 yards.

The buck I drew and skinned, and then wrapped the quartered meat in the hide and placed it into the car. I returned to skin the zebra before jackal or hyena could spoil the hide. I had completed the flaying of the underparts when a grunt caused me to turn. Not far away in a timbered glade stood two cheetahs. It needed no second glance to recognize my pet and her small-headed Romeo, stern-faced as usual.

"Gara-Yaka. Come see!" I gave the customary summons.

She made an uncertain move as though to come to me, but instead she turned to her male escort and sniffed at him. He remained still as a statue, aloof, suspicious, and retiring. My cheetah appeared to be torn between her loyalties.

"Come see, come see!" I tried again.

I took a few steps toward them. Gara-Yaka also moved forward a little, looking back reproachfully at the shy male. Then she ran to me. She greeted me with a joyful "Yunkh." There was much face-rubbing and many playful nips at my knee. She purred loudly her delight at seeing me and for good measure interspersed the purring with little musical notes.

I tried another friendly move toward Romeo. He now lay beneath a large Y-shaped tree. His look showed his disinterest in my advances, and he yawned with absolute boredom. I wanted to make friends with Gara-Yaka's husband, but he remained unfriendly.

He must have thought I was getting too close, so he rose, grunted, and went to the trunk of the tree, scratched at the bark in mock sharpening of claws, jumped into the crotch some 12 to 14 feet up, and then stood there scowling, teeth bared in a snarl that said, "Now don't come any closer!"

I had tried and failed, so I pocketed my pride and accepted the snub with good grace. When I looked back, Romeo had climbed still higher to a better vantage point, all the time keeping an eye on me.

Gara-Yaka was beside the zebra, waiting. I proceeded with the flaying and cut off chunks of meat for her. She held two pieces in her mouth and carried them toward the tree for Lover Boy. Romeo stretched and yawned again, moving about on the thick branches with complete ease and freedom as though he were an arboreal creature. Then he silently leaped down and slunk away beyond the glade. I could not believe that he was not interested in the meat.

Gara-Yaka carried the meat after him, then came back for more. While I sliced a few more chunks she gazed wistfully into the thicket uttering plaintive miaow calls that sounded like "yah-hoo, yah-hoo." She listened intently for Romeo's answering grunt and stood forlorn. Poor girl: she was terribly in love.

I gave her two large pieces of rump which she snatched from my hand; she had never been so ill-mannered! Using her ears as radar discs she plotted position to find Romeo. She ran on what seemed tiptoes in his direction. When he saw the meat he growled his pleasure and joined her, allowing her to rub her face against his, and they tripped

Gara-Yaka in love, brushing against bushes, watching for Romeo

off together. I wondered then if I had misnamed him; his name should have been Gigolo.

Following them into the bush and keeping my distance as I had been warned to do, I noticed that Romeo was a particularly messy eater. Cheetahs are known for this. After his meal, he rolled over like a glutton, completely relaxed. Gara-Yaka sidled up to him and snuggled into the embrace of his forepaws. They lay for a little while, washing each other's face affectionately. I felt like a Peeping Tom and was relieved when they got up and strolled out of sight.

It was clear to me that my cheetah was happy. With a sense of paternal pride I sauntered back to complete the job of flaying the zebra carcass.

chapter 17

A DEEP SNARL stopped me cold in my tracks. I looked toward the half-skinned zebra and found myself staring straight into the fiery yellow eyes of a lioness about to gather herself for a charge at me!

My joy at seeing Gara-Yaka had caused me to be careless. I had left my rifle a few yards from the zebra carcass, so that now it was nearer to the lioness than to me. It would have been absolute suicide had I attempted to regain it, so I jumped for the tree under which my feet seemed to have taken root when I first heard that threatening snarl.

Lions are great bluffers. They enjoy frightening the life out of flesh-and-blood creatures. No normal lion would take on a man when it had its favorite dish, zebra, already served up. That was a comforting thought. But this she-devil had an ugly face and mean yellow eyes. She was not bluffing! She looked up at me perched precariously in the tree, and I vow her teeth matched the yellow of her eyes.

To her way of reasoning, I was the intruder, wanting to steal *her* zebra. How was she to know that I was the rightful owner of the carcass and that all I wanted was its skin.

But I knew all about her! All about those sharp, pointed teeth and powerful ripping claws, frightful weapons now poisoned with decaying flesh. I also knew that she had a spring of 15 yards and a speed of 100 yards under three seconds. No, this one wasn't bluffing. I could see her muscles tense and rippling as she poised her 300-pound body to leap. My arms and legs worked as well as any monkey's, hauling and pushing me higher up out of harm's way just as she arrived under the tree.

She glanced up in a bored way and I shouted at her, hoping to scare her. The yellow eyes blinked as she glared at me, and I knew she could climb the tree—if she really wanted to. The zebra, however, was far more tempting to her, and she returned to the carcass, her swishing tail showing her anger at the disturbance of her meal. She soon settled down to feed.

Hardly had she bloodied her face when she began to look uneasily at the bush. As though on cue, a very fine specimen of a lion appeared and sauntered toward the zebra. The lioness half rose, snarling and ears flattened. She was not moving away fast enough for the King's liking, and he clouted her, sending her cowering to the edge of the bush. This pleased me. He nuzzled the carcass, taking raspy licks here and there, and I could see him slavering with anticipation of a feast.

The lion took hold of the zebra's head and started to drag it away to a place of *his* choice. He could not take it far though, perhaps 30 feet, because the carcass became entangled in a large tree root and all his efforts to dislodge it failed. So he lay down, by this time quite close to my car, and started to gorge himself. At intervals he looked up, his face smeared with blood, to check whether the coast was still clear. When he thought he heard something, he would stretch his great arms across the carcass and wait, open defiance showing clearly on his bloody face. From where I was perched high on the tree I could smell the heavy odor of gore and flesh and, to some extent, the pungent feline odor of the great beast himself.

The lioness must have been this lion's mate, for according to lion table manners, the lord must first have his fill. He was happily occupied with his meal for what seemed hours while she lay panting and drooling in the afternoon heat. This was not the regular lion meal-hour, but the easy meat made it one. Occasionally she would take a look at me to make sure that I was still treed and harmless.

Mid-afternoon, Freddie arrived back with the heavy wheel strapped to his back like a knapsack. He looked around for me while he was wriggling out of the straps. The lioness turned her head and looked hard in Freddie's direction. She started making those "getting ready" movements, gathering herself for the charge. I yelled at Freddie to beware. My tracker was out of the straps in a jiffy and off! The lioness went over to smell the tire. She wrinkled her face, lips pulled up and teeth bared, savoring the air.

At length the lion had had his fill and, with sides bulging, decided to depart. I yelled the information to Freddie, but there was no reply from him. The lioness came back and dug into what was left. By this time the zebra skin was bloodstained and chewed in many parts. Lions tear off strips of meat with the skin, swallowing these with little chewing.

Presently, the male returned. He lay down nearby and began to wash himself. I called to Freddie again. This time he did reply but very tersely. He had seen a large leopard lying downwind. It seemed we were both prisoners and it did me no good to know that leopards are expert tree climbers!

The afternoon wore on to sunset. The lioness finished

Gara-Yaka invited Romeo to supper

loading herself, and when she stood up her stomach bulged so much it hung far down. Then she too decided to leave, taking her lord and master with her.

Now was my chance to clamber down and repossess myself of the rifle. But even before I reached the ground, a volley of coughs sent me scuttling up again as fast as before. Looking down I saw the lime-green eyes of the leopard staring up at me. I hoped it did not have a perverted appetite but instead would prefer its natural food.

The spotted beauty did prefer zebra meat and fed on voraciously into the twilight. I had ample time for wildlife study and also time to reflect on the peculiar consequences of my fluke shot. To top it all, Gara-Yaka invited Romeo to supper with me. But at that moment, I was extricating from my hands and legs thorns which I had not even felt when I had scaled the tree!

The leopard greeted my ward and her lover with warning growls. They replied with their ridiculous cheetah chirping, while working themselves into a feline frenzy. The deeper growls of the leopard were interspersed with throaty spitting and rumbling snarls. Then the now furious leopard hurled himself at my pet(s), sending them scattering into the bush.

The cheetahs did not return, but the lions did. They were accompanied by a shuffling hyena and a couple of jackals. There was a swift rush, a series of rasping snarls and screams in the wake of striking paws. The encounter grew into a savage uproar of quarreling. When at last the skirmish ended, the conversational voices of the proud possessors were those of the lions. They talked and rustled about all night, putting scavengers to flight, while I shivered in the cold on my lofty perch. I thought of Freddie in a similar plight, and I swore the poachers to hell and bitterly cursed the slowly approaching daylight. This relieved my fuming temper but by no means eased the discomfort.

At first light the lions left. Freddie and I took our chance and quickly descended, stiff, bruised, and aching. My strained eyes felt like burning holes in a blanket. But we loosened up our muscles and got our blood circulating again with the exercise of putting on the new tire. And fortunately I had placed the impala meat in the Land Rover, so that we had fresh food to pacify our grumbling stomachs.

Six o'clock in the morning is probably the loveliest part of the day in the bush. The bird population in a grand concert give their thanks to the Creator for their survival of the dark dangers of the night. The sun was bright and already well above the horizon, a welcome warmth after a cramping cold night. The spicy smoke of the campfire together with the aroma of grilling meat was perhaps the most wonderful perfume in the world at this hour. All the hazards of the previous night faded into nothingness. There was the musical bubbling of a pot of strong coffee to complement all the other sounds in this glorious setting.

Then came the discordant notes of a distant "blam, blam"—shooting—like guffaws of derision. The poachers had moved well out of my reach but were still carrying on with their depredations. How I longed to lay my hands on them and to save the game from the swift belching death of their guns. I felt exasperated!

We were about ready to go when I heard the sharp call of a cheetah—Gara-Yaka. She strolled up to us and flopped down seemingly exhausted. Her face showed a happy expression. I patted her and detected a strong wild-feline odor about her. She was very grateful for my affection and licked my hand until the skin tingled under her raspy tongue. Through some reflex dating back to babyhood, she tried to clamber into my lap. But because of her size she repeatedly slipped off. This seemed to annoy her, for she appeared to be longing for sympathy.

Irritably, she scratched to dislodge one of Romeo's fleas which had apparently taken up residence on her. Then she walked away and sat under a tree, moodily gazing into the bush in that searching, faraway manner of hers. She may have had a lover's tiff or been battling with herself to decide on the choice of human company or that of her own wild kind.

I walked up to her and playfully spanked her buttocks. This she used to adore—but not now! She cuffed my arm, slashing my sleeve, and she bit my hand gently but firmly. Her eyes were still focused on some nearby bushes.

I noticed then that hiding under them and blending perfectly into the flecked shadows was Romeo. He was glaring at us with eyebrows knitted.

I gave Gara-Yaka a farewell pat and started back to the car. Immediately Romeo went up to her sniffing possessively at her and licking her head and neck. I saw them walk away—a few feet apart—to continue their honeymoon. The small-headed, hard-faced swain glanced back at me in a supercilious manner as if to say, "Beat it, Buster!"—which, in the circumstances, was the best thing to do.

chapter 18

To wind up the poaching affair I made my report to
the District Commissioner. His face hardened when I told
him of the shots fired at us. He promised immediate reinforcements in the shape of two Land Rovers and four
units of foot patrols who would scour the bush stealthily
—unheralded by engine whines—taking their camp on
donkey-back. From the Back-line northern boundary to
the Limpopo in the south, we cast our wide dragnet.

To allay suspicion I returned to my base camp at Sparkling Waters. Since the poachers' bush-telegraph must
have worked at least as well as mine, we could lose our
chance of capturing them through premature warning.
It was no good just frightening them. Such determined
types had to be severely dealt with or, like a pestilence,
they would keep returning.

Two or three times I went out on my customary patrol
and saw the slow progress of the dragnet. One of the
foot-slogging units had come upon a party of 11 natives,
poachers from the Tribal Territory, living in a camp of
makeshift shacks of branch and grass-mat.

The men were eating and chatting loudly by the camp-

A mound of wild game bones amassed in the backyard of a bushland store

fire when they were surrounded. Two of the party escaped into the bush, taking news of the police unit with them. It was just as well. The remaining nine grimly surrendered after a sprinkling of No. 4 pellets from a shotgun had been fired over their heads. Their camp yielded the remains of 14 impala, two young kudu ewes, five wildebeest, three zebra, and a large kudu bull with enormous horns.

This was a party who, on their own admission, had lived on various parts of our private reserve, snaring, trapping, and killing game at a wholesale rate. They had flayed off every ounce of meat, salted it, and sent it away to the Tribal Territory for sale. They all had a fair amount of money on their persons, doubtlessly their share of the spoils.

There were also piles of bones and skins which they had hoped to sell to white storekeepers. Under a pile of skins there were two elephant tusks weighing about 40 pounds apiece. The men openly admitted that for their traps they had used heavy logs with a spearhead protruding from one end, suspended from high branches above elephant trails. A poor beast would trigger off one of these murder traps and receive a mortal wound from the fallen log. They also had a frightful quantity of wire snares fixed with a running noose for smaller game.

The punishment these poachers received was a form of prison sentence, during which term they would be unfettered, well clothed, and well fed. This "time" was

Captured poacher with a large pair of kudu horns

frequently so much to the prisoners' liking that when it was up they actually begged to be allowed to remain in the police camp rather than leave to return to the drudgery of earning a living.

By now, the rainy season had started. Almost overnight the gray dustbowl of the bushland became transformed into a green paradise. Shoots of fresh leaves and grass pushed through like hairs on a dog's back. The exhilarating smell of rain on dry earth and on sun-heated stones was a sheer tonic. Before the very heavy summer downpours came, which made many of the bushland parts impassable, I had news of the white poachers. The police had located them and summoned my prompt assistance.

With three Land Rovers and two foot patrols we surrounded them, closing in on them gradually. In the distance we heard the frantic popping of rifles, the trumpeting of elephants, and horrible shrieks from human voices: tortured, panic-stricken sounds! A small herd of elephant came crashing through the bush and passed within a few hundred yards of us, totally unaware of our presence. We hurried on and arrived at the poachers' camp which seemed strangely silent. Natives were standing around talking in hushed voices and looking as though they had seen a ghost. They offered no resistance when we moved in on them. It was rather extraordinary to us that there were no white men among them.

One of the natives came forward and eagerly started to tell the gruesome story of what had taken place only a short time before. The party of four white hunters—my poachers—had combed the area in two vehicles and had killed several hundred buck of various types and other animals, including many carnivora wanted for their pelts.

They had used powerful telescopic-sighted rifles and done much of their hunting, despicably enough, by night

These dealt out justice to the poachers

when the beams of their headlights and reflectors blinded the animals, holding them to be slaughtered at will. Trucks at secret meeting places loaded and carted away the carcasses.

Apparently the white poachers had been advised of our approach, and they planned to get some valuable ivory before finally decamping over the border. Thus we were probably instrumental in the denouement, but it was the Law of the Bush that meted out its own grim justice to them.

The dreadful screams we had heard and the trumpeting of the elephants was actually the final act in this drama. For the four, hunting together, had come upon that small herd of elephant which had passed us. In their haste and knowing that we were very close, one of the "hunters" wounded the leader of the herd, a magnificent tusker carrying the nowadays rare load of 180 pounds of ivory.

The wounded tusker screamed and then attacked. All four hunters now concentrated their fire in the direction of the charging colossus, pouring solid-nose bullets into its seven tons of thundering vengeance. The giant's call of pain and fury set the whole herd in motion. They charged the poachers like a phalanx of heavy tanks.

There was no escape! The native assistants and butcher-hands dived for cover, flattening themselves motionless against trees while the whites scattered, terrified, and ran for their lives. Each of the four fleeing poachers was caught by an elephant and mangled in such a frightful manner, as the bodies showed, that the details are best left to the imagination. The Bushland had indeed extracted its due.

We later counted the bulletholes in the great dead tusker and found no less than 34 shots!

With his eyeballs rolling, the native relating the events swore on his ancestors and on the Spirit of the Bush that he and the others would never hunt again. His emotion-choked voice and his trembling limbs told us that he meant every word!

And the great Mudimu who controls the destinies of those who live in the Bushland, and who gives and takes but never makes a mistake, decided, it seems, to aid us further in ridding the private reserve of influences which interfered with the balance of nature.

On our return to camp, we learned from Wilson that he had seen a pack of Kaffir hounds pursuing game. This, of course, required immediate attention, for these half-wild animals were worse in their hunting methods and in their mode of killing than a rampaging leopard in a sheep-fold.

In addition to their carnage, they drove game away from

accustomed home grounds, and thus caused a general dislocation of life and routine similar to that resulting from a bloody insurrection.

In actual fact, the situation was much worse than it appeared at first hearing. While we were driving out to the area concerned, Wilson related how his attention had been attracted by a frightened little buck galloping past him.

Close on the heels of the buck was a dog pack of some 12 to 18 animals. Some of the dogs stopped momentarily when Wilson hailed them in the usual native manner, but the majority of the pursuers ignored him and carried on the chase, tackling their quarry and pulling it down. Avidly they tore the unfortunate antelope to pieces, wolfing the flesh off the still living victim.

Ever since his almost fatal encounter with the bushbuck, Wilson mistrusted the effectiveness of a rifle and preferred to carry the ancestral weapon—an assegai. He approached the feeding dogs and threw sticks and stones at them to drive them off. The fierce brutes, however, turned on him and showed signs of belligerence.

One of the pack then rushed at him with fangs bared. As it leaped at him, Wilson impaled it on the assegai and the attacker crumpled. In the tracks of this brute came the leader of the pack, a great female wolf dog, and Wilson saved himself only by racing away from her at top speed on his bicycle.

From his report, it was obvious that the large pack feared nothing; only the heaviest animals were safe from them. Their presence was a grave threat not only to the game but to Gara-Yaka and even to ourselves. I was pleased that I had brought Piet along for additional support and armed him with a .303.

Wilson guided us to a district that was normally

teeming with buck, some rare species among them. Here we stopped, selecting a good strategic rise from which we could survey a wide expanse through binoculars. The place seemed strangely forlorn and lacking the slowly drifting movement of grazing herds.

I sent Wilson up a giant tree whose scarred trunk bore testimony of attention from the tusks of elephants. From a high crotch he scanned the apron of territory surrounding us. From time to time he reported the passage of one or another animal, giving us a hoof-by-hoof commentary while Piet and I enjoyed a quiet smoke in the shade beneath.

Suddenly Wilson became agitated and hastily slid down in the best baboon fashion. He explained that "wenchus" he was looking, he saw a dog pack moving through the southern wedge and coming in our direction.

We did not have to wait long for developments. The pack appeared a few hundred yards down, in full cry after an impala ewe and her fawn. The ewe was making for a gully which rent a fissure at the bottom of our rise. Her fawn ran beside her like a colored shadow.

The dogs pursued in steeplechase formation, resembling the clutching fingers of some mythical monster of the wild. Then they caught the tired fawn. Some of the hunters remained on the kill, savagely fighting one another for a share, while others pursued the ewe into the gully about 50 yards from us.

I fired three quick shots at the fighting dogs, dropping one with each shot. The dead were pounced upon by their colleagues and torn at! I was picking my next target among these despicable cannibals when sounds of commotion rose nearby. Both Piet and Wilson exclaimed loudly and began jabbering incoherently. I looked around for the cause.

Out of the top crease of the gully came the impala, galloping toward us as though seeking help: one of the dogs was almost at her heels. There was such terror in her eyes that I find my pen too weak to describe it. Yelling to Piet to shoot, I aimed at the dog. Before I could pull the trigger, the dog was at the ewe and killed her with one terrible disemboweling rip of her stomach. Then the dog tore at her throat with indescribable ferocity.

The other pursuers arrived at the kill in an instant, covering the unfortunate carcass like blowflies. Piet was popping away at them with all the pent-up fury of retaliation he had in him, bowling over seven marauders with five shots while I bagged four. The remaining dogs withdrew in swift but sullen reluctance as they became aware that they themselves were being hunted.

A quick count added up to 11 survivors out of the pack's strength of 25. But on closer examination of the dead ones, Wilson insisted that they were not of the same pack he had come across on the previous day. He assured me that he would have recognized the she-wolf-hound leader among the dead or living. This then meant that there was at least another and probably more packs operating in our area.

Wilson dispatched the incapacitated dogs with his assegai, then cut off all their tails to claim the reward from me, or to sell them for "muti." The "undertakers" of the bush would see to the rest. The dead mobsters were mangy, disease-ridden outcasts of the dog world. They were of all sizes, shapes, and colors; many of them were in very bad condition—including two almost hairless ones —and all were covered with open sores. Without exception, they had a colony of large brown fleas—the only friends these dogs had ever had in life.

The unfortunate dogs at one time belonged to natives in

our neighborhood. Most of these rural Bantu—with some notable exceptions—had one ambition in life: to own a very fast dog. For these they would pay an unusually high price in cattle, goats, or produce. But the animals were never prized by their owners as pets; they had to earn their cost and keep by supplying their masters with meat.

They were carefully trained to run down the smaller types of antelope. But as a single dog was insufficient for the job, a small pack was gradually acquired. Now the vicious circle began, for feeding so many mouths would have left the masters no better off; therefore, only scraps were thrown to the animals. The dogs had to find something with which to augment their meager rations, and this they did by catching rabbits which they ran to death.

Strangely these ill-treated and mangy packs kept faith with their owners. The emaciated creatures would fearlessly attack a lion if their master ordered them to do so. For the proud owners, watching this was more fun than tending crops. Now, however, with even their minute drought-ruined crops lost, many of these Bantu headed for the towns or for new pastures and left their dogs to fend for themselves.

I felt sympathy for these poor let-down pariahs who, driven mad with hunger, had gone wild and ganged together in large packs to hunt day and night for themselves. But as they were a menace, I had no choice but to erase them, for by their diabolical killing methods they could soon cause a more wholesale destruction than snares and predators together!

I told both Piet and Wilson of my decision. Understanding the urgency of the matter they endorsed my plan for a clean sweep and suggested the immediate continuation of the hunt until all the dogs had been annihilated. And in this we received a helping hand from a truly unexpected source.

Tracking the spoor of the survivors we came upon them around noon. The dogs were standing in a circle as though in council: they were all facing in and upward. When we spotted them through the matted scrub, we were at first puzzled by their peculiar formation. Testing the wind, we approached cautiously to see what it was about.

The setup we found was most amazing in its composition. Within the dogs' circle stood a ten-foot mamba, the snake reared up so high it swayed to keep its balance. The scene bore a strong resemblance to one out of the ancient past—a druidical ceremony with the slender High Priestess, arms upraised, inspiring a circle of worshipers to adore the sun. A scattered orchestra of brilliantly dressed musicians provided the accompaniment: emerald-spotted doves, barbets, bakbakiries, and shrikes all played their score to create the right atmosphere for the hallowed ensemble.

And then, the magic spell was broken. One of the dogs attended to a demanding flea and then darted in and snapped at the mamba. Its purpose was to draw the snake's attention to itself. Having made the tactical feint and missed the bite, the dog immediately jumped aside and stood at a respectful distance from the now annoyed High Priestess.

The other dogs seemed to take a macabre interest in the slender swaying death, like people who love to be frightened! The haughty Priestess glanced around, darting her tongue at the onlookers. She adjusted her stance, sinking lower, though her head was still a good distance above the ground. Her tongue shot out again in soundless scolding.

A younger and seemingly less experienced dog then

The deadly Priestess—a basking mamba

took up the cue. It rushed in, heedless of caution, and caught the reptile by her middle, shaking the snake as though she were a mere rag doll.

The Priestess bent her body in the shape of a question mark, struck at the foolish but brave dog, and then did a slow, weaving, ballet-like dance. The dog yelped and made an effort at escape from this deadliest creature of all Africa. While the mamba held her fangs firmly imbedded in the dog's neck, the snake was dragged out of position, and this encouraged two more dogs to attack.

But the mamba released her hold and, faster than the eye could follow, turned on the newcomers. Taking slow aim like a marksman, she sank her fangs into one dog's ribs and then into the other's stomach. The fury of an actual outraged priestess could not have been greater than hers, as her neck bulged with the effort of pumping the venom. Poor dogs!

A fourth dog rushed in and grabbed the snake by the neck. This was an old campaigner who knew the ropes. We shuddered with the excitement of the spectacle as the dog twisted the reptile, shook her wildly, and chewed her neck until the snake went limp. Then, still untrusting, the dog jumped aside, and sat down surveying its work with the pride of a victorious general.

This dog I would have spared, for I thought it could have made a wise and valuable pal, but Piet was already sighting his rifle and he fired. He knew better than I that the fugitive would never be caught and tamed again. Piet chalked up another one with his next shot, and I added two more before the four remaining pariahs ran off in as many directions.

The mamba's victims sat with heads drooping, eyes staring and glassy, mouths and muzzles drooling fast. Some six minutes had elapsed since the first strike. The mamba's blood-clotting and neurotoxic poison was taking effect. There is no doubt about its swift and deadly potency: a drop from each fang is poisonous enough to kill a man in 15 minutes. Each of the three dogs had received a multiple of this quantity, and their time was fast running out.

Many a hair-raising story is told at campfires exaggerating the mamba's wicked speed, furious temperament, and terrifying attack on any unfortunate that crosses its path. Admittedly the mamba is a quick, alert, and rather high-strung snake, but actually it would rather get out of a human's way, if it can, than attack. But if suddenly disturbed or badly frightened, it will certainly come on with a vengeance—its black-roofed mouth wide open, its head swaying from side to side high above the ground. Then Heaven help the one in its path!

The fleeing dogs must have come upon the snake while it was sleeping, and awakened, it merely retaliated for the seeming threat to itself. Had the dogs stood still and left a way of escape for the snake, we might not have witnessed this exceptional drama. I know of a fellow hunter who one day came upon a basking mamba. Through sheer fright the man stood in frozen immobility; the snake glided away to its hole right under a bush beside which the hunter stood, touching his trouser leg in its passage.

The first recipient of the bite now keeled over, groaned, and died. The ears of the other two dogs flopped down, and after the animals had made one or two abortive efforts to get up, they too lay down flat in distress and died in painful suffocation. Pangs of guilt assailed me for not having put the dogs out of their misery, but for research purposes I wanted to time the period of the venom's effectiveness.

Blue-tailed flies have the world's most phenomenal sense of smell: they will find a new kill within seconds of the end. They were on the dogs before the last breath was sighed, busy burrowing into the bodies to lay their eggs.

We let the four escapees run. Scattered as they were, the leopards would soon get them. While Wilson extracted the dead mamba's fangs, ceremoniously adding them to his "stock" in the small bead-covered bottle which now dangled around his neck, we heard the "blam" of Freddie's .303 from the direction of our Land Rover.

We found him waiting there to inform me that a commission had arrived in the camp to investigate the death of the four white poachers killed by the elephants.

chapter 19

NEWS OF THIS event spread quickly and far. It frightened away those poachers still lurking in the bush, for natives are very superstitious and they feared the Spirit of the Bush had turned against all poachers. The story of the rough justice meted out also brought many strangers to my camp, especially journalists.

Gara-Yaka had now forsaken Romeo—his usefulness ended—and had, to my delight, returned to the camp.

As I have said, she never made friends readily with casual visitors; she remained conservative and shy despite her inquisitive nature. But those of my friends of long standing of whom she approved were always received with affection, and she loved getting "dressed up" for them. She always knew when I fastened her dog collar around her neck and placed her Tyrolean hat on her head that visitors were expected.

She was a comical sight all dressed up in her Sunday-best. Needless to say, all who saw her, with her mildly smiling face, fell in love with her: Every one of my friends knew of her passion for chocolates, sweets, and sodas. Consequently her sweet tooth was well catered to.

She loved getting "dressed up" for visitors

After her purring, miaowing, and leg-brushing greet-
ings were over—she knew how to perform for the rich
rewards—she would receive her chocolates. Holding one
gently in her mouth, she would hop onto her chair and
start munching noisily while we talked "shop," the usual
topic among people who loved the bush.

With the unusual number of visitors now in camp,
Gara-Yaka was in great demand. Under protest she posed
for pictures, tolerated pats, and was generally examined at
close quarters. When she had had enough of all this, she
disappeared into the bush for hours at a stretch.

One young journalist she disliked from the moment of
meeting. He, on the other hand, could only thinly disguise
his nervousness of her. The others teased him mercilessly
for his—er—shyness. And so, in a spirit of bravado, to prove
that he was no more afraid of the cheetah than they were,
he determinedly walked up to Gara-Yaka.

He was, unfortunately, holding a cup in his hand because of the shortage of glasses. Knowing of Gara-Yaka's distrust of cups ever since her serious illness when the cup meant medicine—which she loathed—I warned him. Thinking this a part of the conspiracy against him and heated by his cupful of liquid courage, he continued to advance. She held up a paw like a policeman on traffic duty indicating "Stop!"

But the man ventured still closer. The cheetah snarled and lashed out with a swift downward cuff; her inch-long nails ripped away his left trouser leg, leaving a crimson gash for all to see. Although she was often provoked, this was the first time she had been so aggressive against a human. Her action certainly had a staying effect on the others.

In the appropriated dog basket, now her "furniture"

My friends and I often analyzed Gara-Yaka and decided that she was passionate, sensitive, and capricious. She could lie eating, purring happily and loudly, and then the next instant the purr would turn into a snarl or a growl. A few seconds later she would purr again, having completely forgotten what had irritated her.

Like most pets and also like most unfettered animals, she was a creature of habit. Everything had a place and there she expected to find it. A very tidy pet! She owned the basket now, a wicker chair, and a leather collar and a hat. When we went out on patrol together—sometimes for days at a stretch—her "furniture" and personal effects had to go too. She was not at all concerned with the comfort of anybody else so long as she was made to feel "at home." Gara-Yaka was high-strung like some dogs, and subject to moods like most domestic cats.

Part of her daily routine was a long walk in the bush. She loved smelling the odors and scents that lingered there, so much so that when she tested the air, I also tried to emulate her. We could smell water, the warm green grass and undergrowth, dry leaves under trees, the mustiness of decay. I learned to find by smell where buck, zebra, or elephant had recently fed or lain-up. Even shimmering heat waves had a smell, oppressive yet unforgettable. We could get the smell of wood-smoke downwind from our camp a mile away, brought to us on a playful breeze. Until these unsung glories of the bush have been experienced, life is incomplete. And these are the only things in the vast Bushland that will remain imperishable.

About ten weeks had passed since Gara-Yaka's "tryst" with Romeo. She was now heavy in whelp. It was one of those oppressively hot afternoons; the shimmering silver heat lay trembling in translucent layers. The mother-to-be was exceptionally restless. She kept scenting the air and wanting to go into the bush. I wondered if her time had come. When I realized that she was really determined to go, I asked a visiting friend to accompany us, perhaps to assist with the birth. We started off.

My cheetah first investigated one side of the track and then crossed over to find out what was on the other side. She tested every bush and tree, her nose working ceaselessly. She was probably seeking a suitable lair. At short intervals she would look back to check that we were still following. About a mile ahead, she loped forward a little and mewed. From a gnarled tree a cheetah jumped to the ground. It was Romeo. They greeted each other with their noses while they uttered low intimate sounds. Romeo had apparently been hanging around the camp, keeping his distance but yet curious to find out how the unborn family was progressing.

The two cheetahs walked off together—I could almost say hand in hand—to a small clearing in the thick scrub. My friend and I followed close in their wake. Romeo departed, perhaps to bring food for his wife. A little later we saw Gara-Yaka prick up her cup-shaped ears; she looked very perturbed.

There was a rustle in the undergrowth, and first the face and then the tawny body of an almost adult lioness emerged. She was followed by another golden body; together they slowly walked toward Gara-Yaka. There was no mistaking those Beatnik faces: they belonged to my cheetah's pet aversions, Sheila and Moll! Now they started to close in on Gara-Yaka, mischief and menace showing clearly in their action.

My cheetah was taken completely off guard and made an attempt to come to us. The two Beatniks charged down on her swiftly. They cut off the cheetah's way of escape

Sheila and Moll charged down on Gara-Yaka

by encircling her. There seemed to be an intent lust-to-kill in their attitude toward my pet.

Before I could think of a plan to assist Gara-Yaka, a fast and savage struggle ensued with all the odds on the lions' side. I knew the cheetah would come off second best, for at no time could she hope to be a match for one lioness of this size, let alone two! They possessed a much more effective killing apparatus in their armor.

For the first time, I saw Gara-Yaka using her dewclaws. Her thumbs, situated well up on the back of her fore-paws held these, the only cat-like claws she possessed. They were curved scimitars, jutting out horizontally when she slashed out in defense or attack. They also provided a firm hold with which to bring a quarry down. She was now using these formidable needle-sharp ripping hooks with good effect. Sheila and Moll were forced to regard her with more respect.

Indeed, so spirited was her reaction to their attack that

Gara-Yaka managed to disengage herself partly from their pincers and made another attempt to run off. But the two females again charged, now roaring in anger, and again succeeded in cutting off escape. Sheila, the heavier one, brought her massive arms into play, mercilessly mauling my cheetah—despite her fierce resistance—and Moll kept running to the cheetah's back to attack her from there. In every respect, the attack was brutal and unfair.

We were unarmed, and even if I had had a gun, I could not have used it for fear of hitting Gara-Yaka. My hat, as usual, was all I had to hurl at the aggressors. I hurled it into the melee; the lions hesitated, surprised. I found a few stones and let them fly at the Beatniks. But these had no effect, for they had recovered from their first surprise and now attacked in earnest, completely ignoring me.

What could I do? They were set on killing my pet!

Sheila forced to regard Gara-Yaka with more respect, while Moll ran to attack her from the back

Armchair strategists may criticize my apparent want of
activity, but given the urgent conditions and the lack of
warning, I had no time to plan.

My friend and I took hold of a large dead thorn bush,
one of many littering the ground, and using it both as
shield and weapon, we waved and thrashed it about as we
entered the arena. Our foolhardy act was born of sheer
desperation. The fight broke up, and the lionesses loped
off, grunting, into the bush.

Gara-Yaka lay cowed on the ground, panting hard and
bleeding from her deep wounds. She was in great distress.
I stroked her head and tried to comfort her with the soft
words she loved, but there was no response. Once or twice
she tried to get up but collapsed at my feet. Her breathing was slow, and she felt cold to the touch. I feared she
would die. Then there came the welcome sound of dogs
barking. Freddie and Piet had heard the growls and roars
and came to investigate.

We improvised a stretcher of my bush-jacket and placed
Gara-Yaka on it. Two of us supported her body underneath
and the other two carried the stretcher. She snarled and
spat but I felt she knew that we were trying to save her.
After a while she lay quite still, uttering little moans. We
hurried on but not without difficulty.

Back in my hut we placed her gently on my bed and
treated her wounds to prevent infection from the poisonous
claws of the lionesses. She began to writhe and grunt.
Some of the sounds were almost human. I wondered if
she had sustained internal injuries and desperately
searched my mind for a remedy in such event.

Freddie and Piet had gone to fetch water, and while my
friend and I rummaged through the medicine chest, we
heard Gara-Yaka utter a pathetic cry. Wheeling around
we saw that a cub had been born. It was dead! We stood

by the bedside very dispirited while two more babies arrived. They were both, thank God, alive.

I wanted to move Heaven and earth to help my cheetah survive the dreadful ordeal, but I could only stroke her head and talk to her encouragingly. Strangely enough, she seemed to respond and attended quite ably to the needs of her newborn cubs. For days we nursed mother and children, giving them tireless attention and love. My pet made a complete recovery and her face glowed with motherly pride.

On the night of the fight and on several successive nights the family of Sheila and Moll came to serenade us, or at least so it appeared. In actual fact they were giving tongue in lion language to another pride that was encroaching on their territory. The serenade started with a solo, and then members of the family joined in, until the earth seemed to tremble. The invaders replied very effectively to the warnings, and the Prodigal and his family had a pawful of trouble.

chapter 20

ALL THIS TIME a new drought persisted, but Gara-Yaka's two babies were blissfully ignorant of the famine that was ravaging the area. The two gray fur-balls suckled and slept and grew fat while the summer rains failed in their fullness and water holes dried up. The river beds once more became desolate and empty. Even the great Limpopo was now subdued. From a river deserving a broad line on maps it had become a third-rate provincial watershed with sluggish ribbons of sand. In many parts its beaches resembled a windswept eroded desert, which contributed little water for the 450-mile journey into the Indian Ocean.

The hitherto plentiful game were beginning to suffer frightfully from little shade, sparse fodder, and very poor water. Many a young fawn perished for lack of mother's milk. Only the meat-eaters waxed sleek and fat: I had never seen lions, hyenas, jackals, and the lesser cats in better shape. It seemed that for them only did those hot ill winds blow any good.

We worked ceaselessly on creating new watering places where our thirst-tortured animals could satisfy their vital

174

need. But because of the heat and glare we could work only from dawn to mid-morning and then again at dusk.

What we saw happening to the game was stark and terrifying. One of our herds of eland was so weak from hunger and thirst that once these animals lay down to rest, they just could not get up again. Herds of wildebeest lay dead and dying, until even the scavengers could not cope with the carrion littering the ground.

With the drought the position of the decimated antelope population became grim. The balance of nature had indeed been upset and the weakened buck were very vulnerable to the suddenly numerous and very fit carnivores. To top it all, lions became finicky and preferred to make a fresh kill rather than help themselves to what was "laid on."

We knew that each lion needed a kill on an average of every fourth or fifth day, and so with roughly 100 lions to 50 square miles of the private reserve, it meant the slaughter of nearly 600 buck every month! I therefore began contemplating the necessity of thinning out some of the carnivores. With some reluctance I decided to weed out 10 per cent of the lion population. Maybe Sheila . . . and Moll perhaps . . . and some of the young busters who had no responsibilities or social status.

Knowing the address of friend Prodigal southeast of my camp, I determined to pay my first call there. By Land Rover we started on the journey toward His Majesty's territory. I had no vain, unbecoming thoughts of revenge on my mind; I just found myself obliged to perform a distasteful task. Sheila and Moll with their turbulent temperaments and their assaults on Gara-Yaka—not without success—were bound to play an important part in game killing.

The sky was an intense blue and the sun was beating down mercilessly on all in the bush. Though bothered by the heat, flies, and dust, I was somehow deep in

Languid Lily and her calf. Checked suit, high heels, and make-up

thought. But all at once we forgot lions, buck, and the queer ways of Nature, for rising from the stunted trees like a distinguished landmark grazed a solitary giraffe. A rare find indeed! This was the first giraffe I had seen in this area.

Years ago, in the days of the vast herds, there may have been hundreds of these odd creatures here, like the hundreds which still thrived five-score miles to the east. We heartily welcomed this seemingly stray wanderer as one Very Important Person.

But our arithmetic was wrong, for under her we saw a baby giraffe looking about with the delicate innocence of a child. A glorious little creature. While the calf suckled, the mother nonchalantly browsed on dry branches and other substances of only she knew what, moving with awkward grace from bush to bush and from tree to tree. In the gentle whiffs of the hot breeze she looked absolutely radiant; her prototype, the slender, long-necked, leggy fashion model of Fifth Avenue, Bond Street, or the Place de la Concorde, could not have bettered her elegance. How well she would have fitted into those places. Her very personality oozed of high fashion. With her sleek tailored checked suit, stiletto-heeled shoes, face beautifully made up with eye shadow, long lashes, and exquisite complexion, she practically cried out to be given a fitting name: Languid Lily, I thought, and thus she was dubbed.

Languid Lily, however, did not share in the enthusiasm we felt for her company. She quickly got our scent and was off like a champion on stilts. I wanted to run after her and the child to beg her to place herself under my protection; after all, this was lion country!

But she haughtily galloped away followed by her bonny babe. Despite this brush-off I felt elated, but I turned my face from the boys, lest they should see how a big-city wolf looked when put firmly in his place by a lady.

Not too far off we barged unannounced through the gates of the Prodigal's royal palace. With his large gold ruff framing his head, His Majesty, like a truly magnificent African potentate, was reclining in his scrub sitting room a few feet off the beaten track. Since our last meeting he had, it seemed, sired himself a small army of cubs.

Formerly his family numbered seven; it was now double this quantity.

I recognized Moll in the harem-nursery with three lively youngsters, while the two older females both appeared to have chipped in with a pigeon-pair each. Only Sheila remained childless. She sat grumpily, and very much below her status, with two near adult youths in the sunbathing compartment of the palace.

The Prodigal welcomed us unblinkingly, distrustfully, showing in no uncertain manner his quite magnificent set of teeth. He was by no means tense. I spoke a few words to him, explaining the situation man-to-man. His response clearly indicated that I was unwelcome and that he did not care for the uncouth manner of my approach; what's more, the grating of my voice tired him. Regarding me with a studied look of disdain, he opened his jaws in a gaping yawn of dismissal. This was my cue, so I moved back and to the side for a better line of fire.

At this, Sheila and the two youths jumped up and vanished. Since her fight with Gara-Yaka and my bashing of her with the spiky thorn bush, she avoided me like the plague. I had often tried to see her, but the temperamental girl was too cunning for me.

Bluntly now, the whole pride showed their dislike of me. The nursing mothers lifted their heads, cocked to one side, revealing their ivory spikes, in case I had stupidly missed the previous demonstration of their lord's dental equipment. It appeared that none of the family had forgiven me for driving them northward to prevent them from raiding cattle and goats in the south; they did not realize that I was trying to save them from the rifles of ranchers.

The Prodigal heaved himself to his feet, conscious of his eminence, and then raised his lips in displeasure at my prolonged lingering. He clawed up clods of earth with his forepaws, and swore his defiance with a deep thundering roar.

I waited quietly, and eventually he turned away with swing-footed, slow padding steps into the bush, but looked back at me at intervals. What was a man to do? I had a mission to carry out, and so I followed Sheila but kept one eye on the Prodigal. He found an inviting nook near a bush and threw himself down in what seemed to be relaxed luxury. Was he only pretending boredom? I hoped to hear his purring grunt of comfort, but the lord remained belligerent. Luckily, a well-timed diversion attracted his family's attention, and I was all ready to breathe a sigh of relief when I saw the objects of their interest! Then I wanted to cry out in anguish.

For through an open glade came Languid Lily, graceful, sleek, and slender, and, beside her, trotting on rubber legs, her carbon copy. Both mother and child presented a picture of pure delight with their mild-mannered and pretty faces and their Eiffel-tower necks. They were coming downwind, blissfully ignorant of the Royal Family in their path.

Champions of the leonine family claim that lions only kill when the need arises. I have long suspected that lions are wont to ignore this compliment and take their chances according to the dictates of their own whims. I had noted the rounded paunches and expressions of repleteness when we arrived. Yet now with their heads flattened to the ground, bodies suddenly tense, the pride showed that they were bent on making monkeys out of their human classifiers.

My rifle had been ready since our arrival, and now I held its stock in a firmer grip, keeping shameless eyes on the ear-flattened earth-hugging lions. Through the corner of my eye, I saw the giraffes stop. To my horror the calf discovered some new wonder of the great wild bushland and, thrusting out its inquisitive little face, decided to examine its find at closer quarters! It moved away from its mother.

While dithering over what I should do, two low, tawny bodies flashed across my field of vision. Two of the pride had made up their minds to pick on the baby. One was Toothless Annie, a senior wife and mother of twins. She had come by her "handle" when a hysterical grass-eater had kicked her teeth in. The other one was a teen-ager youth not yet named in the bush "Who's Who."

Languid Lily saw them too! Without any hesitation, she countercharged and met Toothless Annie halfway. On impact she started using her weapons. Slashing at the thoughtless Annie with her forefeet, she then turned and kicked at the lioness with the hind ones, hitting fair and square and sending Annie into a mauled heap within seconds. Poor Toothless Annie had not learned from previous experience.

Just then the young hoodlum came up, but slowed down considerably when he witnessed his aunt's fate. With the insolence of youth, he slipped around Languid Lily and made for the little one. But like his aunt, he obviously had no experience with giraffe. Languid Lily brought another weapon into play: with her head, she struck the lion aside and then turned to treat him to some fancy footwork.

Though thick-bellied lions are sluggish, this youngster knew that the odds were against him and so turned and took cover with incredible speed. Peering out from under a protective bush, he now took stock of the long-legged lady nemesis. But Madame did not appear content with routing him. She advanced on the bush to attack him again.

The young lion, tail drooping, fled some distance to the protection of another bush where he took up a defensive stand. Before the giraffes' luck was too sorely tried and retribution could descend on them, I shot the mischievous lion. Although the show was now over, Languid Lily was surely a marked person. The pride had noted her mode of attack and defense, and as many people know, lions are observant creatures.

The explosive report of the rifle sent every mobile being to flight in seconds. A grunting Prodigal led the exodus, his anger completely forgotten. He called to the nursing mothers to follow, and they answered in low grunts while gathering their respective broods, the tumbling cubs now yapping their disapproval in a high-pitched chorus. It was bedlam until the decks were cleared. By the time I looked for Languid Lily, she must have been miles away with her child.

Both attackers were dead. Toothless Annie had her head blown off by the full force of that hind hoof on her fore-head. It was shameful for an old lioness to be sent to the eternal Hunting Grounds by a seemingly helpless creature like a giraffe, but Annie was a cat, and felines determinedly carry through foolish notions regardless of consequences. The young lion had also been badly injured by the giraffe, but it was the bullet just behind his right eye which had finished him off.

We started a search for Toothless Annie's twin cubs, but apparently the other females of the pride had collected them with their own. Somehow they must have known that the two little ones were now orphans. Following the pride's spoor we traced them to a ravine. Through bin-oculars I saw them, and they all appeared to be totally unaffected by the past events. All seven cubs were being well cared for by the remaining two lionesses. Moll was suckling three, and four were with the other senior lady.

Honoring the remaining youth with his royal presence,

the Prodigal lay a little way off from the nursery and
seemed to be quietly discussing the loss of two of his
family. I realized then that Sheila was conspicuous by her
absence. This puzzled me.

Sharp-eyed Piet gave me a nudge and pointed with his
face to the side of the slope. Through the long grass came
Sheila, making straight for the family gathering. She
greeted the old lady first, then her sister Moll, and after
that, all the cubs in turn. She was received with lavish
signs of delight, but the Prodigal ignored her.

Sheila settled down a few feet away with the womenfolk
and children and appeared to chat with them in subdued
tones. Two of the cubs, probably the orphans, waddled
up to her on shaky legs and tried her unsuccessfully for a
feed. She gave a wide yawn of obvious unhappiness and
washed the cubs lovingly with a great display of nuzzling
their undersides, licking, and placing a very large paw on
their small backs to anchor them for further cleansing. I
was impressed by these signs of her motherly instincts and
guessed at her longing for cubs of her own.

At the risk of censure from Gara-Yaka for my neglect of
her, I took time off to trail Sheila and to watch how she
and the Prodigal would resolve their differences. I got my
answer sooner than I expected.

There was an old bachelor lion north of the Majali whom
I had seen a few times but did not know very well. Each
time we met, I noted his good physique and his rugged
face set in a well-combed mane which emphasized his
heavy features. My pate being completely bald, I was
tickled to a smile by his beautifully barbered dark hair.
Indeed, I was intrigued not only by his hair style but by
his dead-pan face and pale green killer eyes. I watched
with respect his wag-humped sinuous walk in which there
was something of the deadly stealthiness of an old Wild

West gunslinger. Though he was well past kid age, I could not help but name him "Billy the Kid."

One day Sheila and Billy the Kid met, and their life-cords became entangled. I believe it was love at first sight. I could see how Sheila fought with her conscience to retain the respectability of her marriage to the Prodigal. But love had the upper hand.

As a consequence, she succumbed to the secret and fierce wooing of Billy. Our friend was now not only intruding into the pride's territory but into their private lives too. Naturally he faced heavy penalties. Lions are creatures with a strong social sense, a flair for etiquette and order of rank. They are also pretty touchy in property matters, as all humans are.

No self-respecting lion could face his lady love again

Sheila took occasional French leave

Sheila and Billy sunning in the shine of their love

if a shameful thing happened to him; therefore, Billy the Kid carefully minded his step and picked his hours for stolen love while the pride relaxed replete and slept. "Tell a woman she's fair and soon she'll turn fool," goes an old adage, and by Billy's advances he must have known this, for I saw him murmuring sweet nothings close to her ear.

Sheila became so enamored of him and so alienated from her family that she left the pride. Soon I saw her kill for him and observe the age-old lion ceremonial of taking for herself only some of the blood and soft underparts; she opened the kill for him and let him have the first feed and naturally the lion's share.

The old rake seemed to want to wheedle his way into the pride, but neither Sheila nor the Kid had taken into account the Prodigal and his standing. The Prodigal was an absolute master of his household and his magnificent proportions had given him additional strength and confidence. There was aristocracy in his every line—true bush royalty—and behind him his whole family stood solidly.

The fatal hour of reckoning between the two rivals struck at high noon one day when all lions should have been asleep in carefully chosen spots of shade, breathing the sweet-scented searing air. It was the "Silent Hour." Hardly a living thing stirred in the hot midday sun, unless of course mad dogs and Englishmen, but they were in any case not expected to be present at this battle royal.

There came Billy the Kid with an ersatz swagger of his lean buttocks. Though his broad shoulders rippled with muscles, there was a slight hollow in his back as though the weight of his momentous intrusion rested there.

The battle itself was a tremendous clash of fangs, claws, and exceptional power. The fury of it was boldly told by the disturbed earth and broken vegetation. Like a Highland Clan, the whole pride fought the intruder, tarring him with earth and feathering him with bites and claw marks. They ran Billy the Kid out of the territory.

The Prodigal, outraged and furious, dealt out punishment to the wayward Sheila, who lost a canine tooth and had two toes complete with claws bitten off her right forepaw. Then she was expelled from the pride. The bush law, from which our own laws had been derived, once again exacted justice. May it never cease to exist! With so many injuries, Sheila would find survival a problem, and I wondered how she would make out.

That night, when the evening star rose through the heat of campfire smoke, the earth and vegetation exuded strange

The Prodigal. The day of reckoning had been ordained

and exotic smells, as the Prodigal attended to his wounds-of-honor while encircled by his family.

I too was attending to my wounds, but these were not received in battle. They had been caused by hundreds of infinitesimal bush-ticks which I had picked up in my trailing of Sheila and Billy the Kid. These minute insects burrow into the pores of the skin and suck one's blood, causing itching and irritation. I scratched like a monkey, here, there, and just anywhere!

My whole body was covered by pea-sized spots and my game scouts likened me to Gara-Yaka. The comparison greatly amused them. In extreme discomfort I had a good

Billy the Kid. The fatal hour struck at high noon

retort and asked them how many spots they thought our cheetah had. Their answers varied between 200 and 300. Now it was my turn to laugh, for unknown to them I had actually counted Gara-Yaka's spots most carefully, and they amounted to exactly 1,967!

The gorgeous spotted lady in question lay beside me near the fire sniffing at my discarded clothing and shoes. She snarled angrily when she got the scent of Sheila's amputated toes in my pocket.

Fortunately Gara-Yaka's cubs began to squawk and she left the fire to see to them before matters resolved into an ugly scene.

chapter 21

SEVERAL WEEKS after the birth of the cubs, I had a strange dream in which I saw Mulembe coming for me with his jaws open wide. The cry of a nightjar woke me from the frightful predicament. It was still dark, but I noticed a touch of saffron in the east. The shadowed velvet of the night started to pale to gray. A few stars still twinkled brightly, and the pure, crisp morning air made me feel good to be alive.

It was again time to take water-level readings and to report on the condition of grass and veld, so I decided to go south at daybreak. Gara-Yaka had not been out since the big fight and by her recent restlessness I could tell she was longing for a good run. I took her on this trip and Freddie came too. Piet stayed behind to take care of the cubs.

The silence was almost tangible when we left, except for the sounds of one or two early birds greeting the dawn. The gray shapes of guinea-fowl speeding across our path in jerky runs was the only movement we saw at this early hour. Then the sky gradually became lighter, and the sun rose in a splendor of scarlet and gold, flooding the Bushland generously. Small and large types of grass-eaters stood on and off the path watching the Land Rover pass. Some lay, already full-bellied, blissfully unconcerned with the world.

The recent rains had left pools in cavities on the ground, and around these rich vegetation had sprung up interspersed with the pattern of vividly hued flowers. No carpet, hand-made, could have competed with this magic weave of the Creator.

There was a fair flow in the river, but the water was well below the average volume for midsummer. Large sand banks showed above the level. Having completed my chores, I walked along the shore toward a turn where the river bed bellied out to form a bay. The day was hot and the water in the bay looked tranquil and inviting. I thought a dip might be enjoyable.

My attention was arrested by the loud grunting of a hippo bull calling its mate and offspring from the deep water of the bay. Careful scanning of the surface revealed the sinister shape of a large crocodile snout. The hippo bull continued its call, its "ho, haw-haw," sounding like a fat man's beer-filled guffaw in a tavern.

My longing for a bath immediately evaporated when I sighted the large crocodile. It could not have been any other but friend Mulembe. He must have realized that he had been spotted by the hippo, and with as much dignity as he could muster, the Sacred One withdrew.

I watched this living, armored submarine slowly cruise toward a sandspit in the middle of the river, the water rippling before his protruding eyes and nostrils. The Limpopo forms a natural boundary between Bechuanaland and the Transvaal for over 200 miles here. The sandspit in the middle was no-man's land; Mulembe headed there.

For only a moment, I turned to see where Gara-Yaka was, and then a sudden disturbance recalled my attention to the river. A spray of sand shot up at the edge of the steep bank. Mulembe uttered a throaty roar. Calling Freddie and Gara-Yaka I raced along the bay to where the shore was just over 20 yards from the sandspit. There was Mulembe, lying as still as a fallen tree trunk. Around his forequarters a python was coiled, holding the armor-plated body in its vise-like grip.

When he recovered from the initial shock, the crocodile started to wriggle and jerk, throwing his forepart into the air while his massive saw-edged tail lashed furiously against the sand in an effort to free himself. His great jaws snapped again and again, probably at the unseen head of his equally giant adversary. The steel-tough coils of the snake tightened more and more, squeezing the resistance out of Mulembe, and locking him in a death-grip.

The sight of the struggle between these king-sized reptiles was weird and uncanny. Mulembe's hind legs plowed up piles of sand in a vain effort to reach the water, but with his forelegs imprisoned, the effort was doomed. But when one moving coil lashed over the crocodile's head, Mulembe snapped at it with spiky-toothed jaws which almost bit through. It was a near thing for the snake.

With quick, undulating movements, the python re-arranged its coils. The power of its new grip made Mulembe gasp, and he released the captured coil. I remembered the small crocodile and its uneven fight with Mulembe. By a quirk of fate, the unmerciful monster was now in a similar position. He managed to turn over on his back in a roll, his tail frantically flailing.

For one fleeting second the great Mulembe lay dead-still; then with renewed energy and a final effort to extricate himself, he brought forward his tail for leverage. This desperate move was his downfall: even I could see the grave error of this tactic.

Mulembe's haunt, the hippo pool

Some stones from Mulembe's stomach in a Tswana hand-woven basket

In a flash, the python had Mulembe's tail caught in a ring formed by the thin end of its own. Like a wrestler it bent the tail forward, squeezing it against the crocodile's side.

We heard a crack as Mulembe's spine snapped under the scaly hide. The monster went limp. With cool deliberation the victor further tightened its muscular coils, cracking, it seemed, every bone in the crocodile's body. And the battle was over.

A pause followed and all was silent. Like a dragon of fantasy, the python started to unwind itself with slow grace from the shapeless mass and glided away, leaving behind a furrow tinged with red, for blood was oozing from its wound. We stood, filled with awe, and watched as the tail disappeared into the tangled growth on the other side. Only then did we venture closer to the shattered body of the former terror of the river. I could not help but feel a little sad at the passing of the majestic Mulembe, for it was because of him that I came to own Gara-Yaka.

My cheetah crept up to the recumbent killer of her dam and instinctively growled at him. When she noticed no response, she cuffed at his snout, and it was then that I spotted some interesting-looking stones lying in the sand where the snout rested. I picked up one of the stones.

It was a good-sized *blue-white diamond* which I judged to be of considerable value.

The rest were quartz, chalcedony, and coarse agate. The stones had been disgorged by Mulembe when the python squeezed him in the death-grip.

Crocodiles always carry a number of stones in their stomachs to aid their digestion. Ostriches are well known to do the same, and they often pick up diamonds, being attracted by the sparkle. Even the gizzard of a chicken is usually filled with tiny stones and grit.

I thought about all this and decided to open up Mulembe to search for more stones. Freddie and I had great difficulty in cutting through the tough hide, but eventually we succeeded. The foul stench nearly bowled us over when we eviscerated the monster.

On opening the stomach we found a large quantity of stones embedded there: all sizes, shapes, and colors. When we had washed away the mess, we gasped, for among them we had indeed found a treasure trove. Poor Mulembe had paid handsomely in death for his misdeeds!

Now in my mind's eye I could see the strong, high fence that I would erect around my own private reserve. My dream could now become a reality. Gara-Yaka with her cubs, all the other wild animals and birds would live there happily and unafraid of poachers' guns and snares. This was what fate had willed that day when I tried to rescue Gara-Yaka's mother at this very river's edge.